Dante's *Vita Nuova:*

A Translation and an Essay

Mary Ann Geadon

DANTE'S

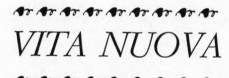

VITA NUOVA

A Translation and an Essay

by Mark Musa

A NEW EDITION

Indiana University Press

Bloomington & London

Published in Canada by
Fitzhenry & Whiteside Limited, Don Mills, Ontario
Library of Congress catalog card number: 72-79905

ISBN: 0-253-31620-0 cl.   0-253-20162-4 pa.

Manufactured in the United States of America

3   4   5   77 78

For
Anna Granville Hatcher
*who once told me that Scholarship is the
drama between the scholar's bright idea
and the seductive and implacable evidence.*

CONTENTS

PREFACE

᷿᷿᷿᷿᷿ THE *Vita Nuova*, one of Dante's earliest works, is a combination of prose and poetry. There are thirty-one poems inserted into the prose text according to the following arrangement:

I	....	XVI	sonnet	XXIX	....
II	....	XVII	....	XXX	....
III	sonnet	XVIII	....	XXXI	canzone
IV	....	XIX	canzone	XXXII	sonnet
V	....	XX	sonnet	XXXIII	unfinished
VI	....	XXI	sonnet		canzone
VII	sonnet	XXII	sonnet	XXXIV	sonnet
VIII	sonnet		sonnet	XXXV	sonnet
	sonnet	XXIII	canzone	XXXVI	sonnet
IX	sonnet	XXIV	sonnet	XXXVII	sonnet
X	sonnet	XXV	....	XXXVIII	sonnet
XI	....	XXVI	sonnet	XXXIX	sonnet
XII	ballad		sonnet	XL	sonnet
XIII	sonnet	XXVII	reduced	XLI	sonnet
XIV	sonnet		canzone	XLII	....
XV	sonnet	XXVIII	....		

The originality of the *Vita nuova* consists not in the mixture of prose and verse (a device used by Boethius in his *Philosophiae Consolatio* and, a century before him, by Martianus Capella), but in the functional relationship between the two: it seems to be a fact that the *Vita nuova* is the first work of fiction including both prose and poetry, in which the prose serves the purpose not only of offering a continuous narrative but also of explaining the occasion for the composition of each of the poems included.

Also significant is the chronological relationship between the composition of the poems and that of the prose narrative, which reflects the way in which the author has adapted to a new purpose some of his earlier writings. For scholars generally agree that when Dante, some time between 1292 (that is, two years after the death of Beatrice) and 1300, composed the *Vita nuova*, most, if not all, of the poems that were to appear in the text had already been written. The architecture of the work, then, consists of selected poems arranged in a certain order, with bridges of prose between them, bridges that serve (with the exception of the "essays" represented by Chapters XXV and XXIX) primarily a narrative function: to describe those events in the life of the protagonist, which supposedly inspired the poems. By offering in this way a narrative background, the author was able to make their meaning clearer—or, perhaps, to change their original meaning or purpose.

Thus, the first canzone, "Donne ch'avete intelletto d'amore," though its beauty is independent of its position in the work, owes entirely to the preceding narrative its dramatic significance as the proclamation of a totally new attitude adopted by the poet-lover. Again, the poem in Chapter XXVII describing the disequilibrium of the lover's *spiriti* caused by the presence of his lady is insignificant in itself, and treats a theme frequently recurring in the book; but the author's decision to place this familiar theme immediately after Chapter XXVI (a most strategic choice of location, as the reader will come to see) invests it with dynamic overtones which could determine, in a most important way, the message of the *Vita nuova* itself.

Now, just how much of the narrative prose is fiction we shall never know: we can never be sure that a given poem actually arose from the circumstances related in the preceding prose. A few critics believe that all of the events of the narrative reflect biographical truth; most, fortunately, are more skeptical. But it goes without saying that in reading the *Vita nuova* we must suspend our skepticism and accept as "true" the events of the narrative. For only by doing so can we perceive the significance that the author attributed to his poems by placing them where he did. And most critics of the *Vita nuova* seem to be agreed that in interpreting this work as a piece of literature, in seeking to find its message, the reader must try to forget the biographical fact that any given poem may have been written before Dante could know the use he would make of it later on. And no serious critic, if puzzled by the inclusion of a certain poem in the book, or by its position, would dare to brush aside the problem by saying to himself that, after all, Dante had some old poems in his desk drawer that he was determined to use, somehow.

Still, the critic's knowledge of the earlier existence of the poems does constitute an insidious danger, of which often he may not be aware, making it difficult for him to face squarely the problems that the poems may offer in their new setting. It is this knowledge, I believe, that has prevented critics from studying the individual poems and their position in the work as carefully as they should. It is most important that Dante has chosen to include any particular poem and to place it where he did; it could have appeared somewhere else, or of course, have been omitted. The critic must realize the conclusive importance of Dante's choices, and he must seek to discern Dante's intention through very careful analysis.

This point will be stressed more than once in my *Essay;* in fact, my study differs from others mainly because, whenever a poem is analyzed, it is considered against the background of the narrative as reflecting what happens in time—from the moment the protagonist as a young child meets the child

Beatrice, to the moment when he, as a grown man, decides that what he has written is unworthy of her.

The earlier edition of my translation of the *Vita nuova* included an Introduction, which was mainly an interpretation of the significance of the book. In the present volume that Introduction has been replaced by a much longer study, different from the previous attempt at analysis in two important ways. First, of the three chapters of my "Essay," two are concerned with problems which do not directly involve the moral message of the *Vita nuova:* the first chapter ("Patterns") has a rather novel approach, and concerns the structure of the work and the artistic ingredients that go into its making. In the second ("Aspects") I take up a well-known, much debated problem: the identity or the representational value of the figure called "Love," who appears in various guises on the stage of the lover's imagination. It is in the third chapter ("Growth") that the teaching of Dante's *Vita nuova* is investigated, with results that are considerably at variance with the ideas I had previously expressed: indeed, in one important sense, they are radically opposed to them. In this chapter I seek to explain in considerable detail, and to justify as convincingly as possible, my new convictions about the purpose of this extraordinary little book.

TRANSLATOR'S NOTE

☙ ☙ ☙ ☙ ☙ In this translation of the *Vita nuova*, as in the one I published fifteen years ago, I have avoided the use of rhyme in the poetry, continuing to render the Italian original in English blank verse. My reasons for not submitting to the tyranny of rhyme in translating Dante's poetry have been presented in the Foreword to my recent translation of the *Inferno;* there I also expressed my ideas about what faithfulness to the original should mean for the translator of poetry.

It might seem that the problem would be much less difficult for the translator of prose. I should say that it is less complicated, but is, nonetheless, difficult if the original text was composed centuries ago, when the patterns of prose style were quite different from those of our own time. There is no doubt about it: to the reader who goes from modern Italian prose to the prose of the *Vita nuova* the older style seems stilted and verbose; and the reader always seems to be in the midst of a dependent clause, or to have just escaped from one, or to be about to enter into another. Yet it would be a sacrilege to reduce Dante's elaborate prose periods to simpler predications. On the other hand, should one offer the reader a translation with sentences that may be tedious to read, and language which will strike him as unnatural? To find a happy compromise is not easy, and this is particularly true of the narrative prose of the *Vita nuova*. The suggestion of "stuffiness" that would be unavoidable in a translation of a philosophical work such as Dante's *Convivio* would certainly be tolerated by all readers, and perhaps even enjoyed. It is less enjoyable in a narrative; and

Dante's narrative style is at times indistinguishable from the expository style of his *Convivio*. Thus, in Chapter XXII of the *Vita nuova*, after announcing the death of Beatrice's father, he continues:

> Since such a departure is sorrowful to those who remain and who have been friends of the deceased; and since there is no friendship more intimate than that of a good father for a good child, or of a good child for a good father; and since her father, as is believed by many and is the truth, was exceedingly good—then it is clear that this lady was filled with bitterest sorrow.

Sometimes, it is true, careful study will reveal that what seems at first glance to be unpardonable pedantry was inspired by the deepest artistry. To mention one instance: seven times the city of Florence is designated by the phrase "the above-mentioned city" (*la sopradetta cittade*); just why this legalistic periphrasis was chosen (and why the city is never called by name) I shall attempt to explain in terms of the message of the *Vita nuova* itself. But many times the explanation for Dante's stylistic choices must be sought in certain very personal predilections of the author which are generally not shared by writers of narrative. Surely whatever it was (and this matter will be discussed) that inspired the author of the *Vita nuova* to attach to most of his poems a minutely precise explanation of their content—thereby anticipating, though for a different purpose, his procedure in the *Convivio*—helps explain the choice of his prose style in general.

If the reader believes, as he must, that Dante's prose style, more appropriate to exposition than to narrative, represents a deliberate choice by a man of genius, he will probably appreciate the goal I have set myself: to respect every detail of Dante's sentence structure as far as it is possible to do so within the limits set by the patterns of English idiom.

The *New Life*

I

~~~~~~~~~~ IN MY BOOK OF MEMORY, in the early part where there is little to be read, there comes a chapter with the rubric: *Incipit vita nova*.[1] It is my intention to copy into this little book the words I find written under that heading—if not all of them, at least the essence of their meaning.

II

Nine times already since my birth the heaven of light had circled back to almost the same point, when there appeared before my eyes the now glorious lady of my mind, who was called Beatrice even by those who did not know what her name was. She had been in this life long enough for the heaven of the fixed stars to be able to move a twelfth of a degree to the East in her time; that is, she appeared to me at about the beginning of her ninth year, and I first saw her near the end of my ninth year. She appeared dressed in the most patrician of colors, a subdued and decorous crimson, her robe bound round and adorned in a style suitable to her years. At that very moment, and I speak the truth, the vital spirit, the

1. "The new life begins."

one that dwells in the most secret chamber of the heart, began to tremble so violently that even the most minute veins of my body were strangely affected; and trembling, it spoke these words: *Ecce deus fortior me, qui veniens dominabitur michi.*[2] At that point the animal spirit, the one abiding in the high chamber to which all the senses bring their perceptions, was stricken with amazement and, speaking directly to the spirits of sight, said these words: *Apparuit iam beatitudo vestra.*[3] At that point the natural spirit, the one dwelling in that part where our food is digested, began to weep, and weeping said these words: *Heu miser, quia frequenter impeditus ero deinceps!*[4] Let me say that, from that time on, Love governed my soul, which became immediately devoted to him, and he reigned over me with such assurance and lordship, given him by the power of my imagination, that I could only dedicate myself to fulfilling his every pleasure. Often he commanded me to go and look for this youngest of angels; so, during those early years I often went in search of her, and I found her to be of such natural dignity and worthy of such admiration that the words of the poet Homer suited her perfectly: "She seemed to be the daughter not of a mortal, but of a god." And though her image, which remained constantly with me, was Love's assurance of holding me, it was of such a pure quality that it never allowed me to be ruled by Love without the faithful counsel of reason, in all those things where such advice might be profitable. Since to dwell on my passions and actions when I was so young might seem like recounting fantasies, I shall put them aside and, omitting many things that could be copied from the text which is the source of my present words, I shall turn to those written in my memory under more important headings.

2. "Here is a god stronger than I who comes to rule over me."
3. "Now your bliss has appeared."
4. "Oh, wretched me! for I shall be disturbed often from now on."

III

After so many days had passed that precisely nine years were ending since the appearance, just described, of this most gracious lady, it happened that on the last one of those days the miraculous lady appeared, dressed in purest white, between two ladies of noble bearing both older than she was; and passing along a certain street, she turned her eyes to where I was standing faint-hearted and, with that indescribable graciousness for which today she is rewarded in the eternal life, she greeted me so miraculously that I seemed at that moment to behold the entire range of possible bliss. It was precisely the ninth hour of that day, three o'clock in the afternoon, when her sweet greeting came to me. Since this was the first time her words had ever been directed to me, I became so ecstatic that, like a drunken man, I turned away from everyone and I sought the loneliness of my room, where I began thinking of this most gracious lady and, thinking of her, I fell into a sweet sleep, and a marvelous vision appeared to me. I seemed to see a cloud the color of fire and, in that cloud, a lordly man, frightening to behold, yet he seemed also to be wondrously filled with joy. He spoke and said many things, of which I understood only a few; one was *Ego dominus tuus*.[5] I seemed to see in his arms a sleeping figure, naked but lightly wrapped in a crimson cloth; looking intently at this figure, I recognized the lady of the greeting, the lady who earlier in the day had deigned to greet me. In one hand he seemed to be holding something that was all in flames, and it seemed to me that he said these words: *Vide cor tuum*.[6] And after some time had passed, he seemed to awaken the one who slept, and he forced her cunningly to eat of that burning object in his hand; she ate of it timidly. A short time after this, his

5. "I am thy master."
6. "Behold thy heart."

happiness gave way to bitterest weeping, and weeping he folded his arms around this lady, and together they seemed to ascend toward the heavens. At that point my drowsy sleep could not bear the anguish that I felt; it was broken and I awoke. At once I began to reflect, and I discovered that the hour at which that vision had appeared to me was the fourth hour of the night; that is, it was exactly the first of the last nine hours of the night. Thinking about what I had seen, I decided to make it known to many of the famous poets of that time. Since just recently I had taught myself the art of writing poetry, I decided to compose a sonnet addressed to all of Love's faithful subjects; and, requesting them to interpret my vision, I would write them what I had seen in my sleep. And then I began to write this sonnet, which begins: *To every captive soul.*

> To every captive soul and loving heart
>   to whom these words I have composed are sent
>   for your elucidation in reply,
>   greetings I bring for your sweet lord's sake, Love.
>   The first three hours, the hours of the time
>   of shining stars, were coming to an end,
>   when suddenly Love appeared before me
>   (to remember how he really was appalls me).
>
> Joyous, Love seemed to me, holding my heart
>   within his hand, and in his arms he had
>   my lady, loosely wrapped in folds, asleep.
>   He woke her then, and gently fed to her
>   the burning heart; she ate it, terrified.
>   And then I saw him disappear in tears.

> *A ciascun' alma presa e gentil core*
>   *nel cui cospetto ven lo dir presente,*
>   *In ciò che mi rescrivan suo parvente,*
>   *salute in lor segnor, cioè Amore.*
>   *Già eran quasi che atterzate l'ore*
>   *del tempo che onne stella n'è lucente,*

quando m'apparve Amor subitamente,
(cui essenza membrar mi dà orrore).

Allegro mi sembrava Amor tenendo
meo core in mano, e ne le braccia avea
madonna involta in un drappo dormendo.
Poi la svegliava, e d'esto core ardendo
lei paventosa umilmente pascea.
Appresso gir lo ne vedea piangendo.

This sonnet is divided into two parts. In the first part I extend greetings and ask for a response, while in the second I
describe what it is that requires the response. The second part
begins: *The first three hours.*

This sonnet was answered by many, who offered a variety of
interpretations; among those who answered was the one I call
my best friend, who responded with a sonnet beginning: *I
think that you beheld all worth.* This exchange of sonnets
marked the beginning of our friendship. The true meaning
of the dream I described was not perceived by anyone then, but
now it is completely clear even to the least sophisticated.

IV

After that vision my natural spirit was
interfered with in its functioning, because my soul had become
wholly absorbed in thinking about this most gracious lady;
and in a short time I became so weak and frail that many of
my friends were worried about the way I looked; others, full
of malicious curiosity, were doing their best to discover things
about me, which, above all, I wished to keep secret from
everyone. I was aware of the maliciousness of their questioning
and, guided by Love who commanded me according to the
counsel of reason, I would answer that it was Love who had

conquered me. I said that it was Love because there were so many of his signs clearly marked on my face that they were impossible to conceal. And when people would ask: "Who is the person for whom you are so destroyed by Love?" I would look at them and smile and say nothing.

V

It happened one day that this most gracious of ladies was sitting in a place where words about the Queen of Glory were being spoken, and I was where I could behold my bliss. Halfway between her and me, in a direct line of vision, sat a gentlewoman of a very pleasing appearance, who glanced at me frequently as if bewildered by my gaze, which seemed to be directed at her. And many began to notice her glances in my direction, and paid close attention to them and, as I left this place, I heard someone near me say: "See what a devastating effect that lady has had on that man." And, when her name was mentioned, I realized that the lady referred to was the one whose place had been half-way along the direct line which extended from the most gracious Beatrice, ending in my eyes. Then I was greatly relieved, feeling sure that my glances had not revealed my secret to others that day. At once I thought of making this lovely lady a screen to hide the truth, and so well did I play my part that in a short time the many people who talked about me were sure they knew my secret. Thanks to this lady I concealed the truth about myself for several years and months, and in order to encourage people's false belief, I wrote certain trifles for her in rhyme which I do not intend to include unless they could serve as a pretext to treat of that most gracious Beatrice; therefore, I will omit them all except for what is clearly in praise of her.

VI

Let me say that during the time that this lady acted as a screen for so great a love on my part, I was seized by a desire to record the name of my most gracious lady and to accompany it with the names of many others, and especially with the name of this gentlewoman. I chose the names of sixty of the most beautiful ladies of the city in which my lady had been placed by the Almighty, and composed a *serventese* in the form of an epistle which I shall not include here—in fact, I would not have mentioned it if it were not that, while I was composing it, miraculously it happened that the name of my lady appeared as the ninth among the names of those ladies, as if refusing to appear under any other number.

VII

The lady I had used for so long to conceal my true feelings found it necessary to leave the aforementioned city and to journey to a distant town; and I, bewildered by the fact that my ideal defense had failed me, became extremely dejected, more so than even I would previously have believed possible. And realizing that if I should not lament somewhat her departure, people would soon become aware of my secret, I decided to write a few grieving words in the form of a sonnet (this I shall include here because my lady was the direct cause for certain words contained in the sonnet, as will be evident to one who understands). And then I wrote this sonnet which begins: *O ye who travel.*

O ye who travel on the road of Love,
  pause here and look about
  for any man whose grief surpasses mine.

I ask this only: hear me out, then judge
if I am not indeed
the host and the abode of every torment.
Love—surely not for my slight worth, but moved
by his own nobleness—
once gave me so serene and sweet a life
that many times I heard it said of me:
"God, what great qualities
give this man's heart the riches of such joy?"

Now all is spent of that first wealth of joy
that had its source in Love's bright treasury;
I know Love's destitution
and have no heart to put into my verse.
And so I try to imitate the man
who covers up his poverty for shame:
I wear the clothes of joy,
but in my heart I weep and waste away.

O voi che per la via d'Amor passate,
attendete e guardate
s'elli è dolore alcun, quanto 'l mio, grave.
E prego sol ch'audir mi sofferiate,
e poi imaginate
s'io son d'ogni tormento ostale e chiave.
Amor, non già per mia poca bontate,
ma per sua nobiltate,
mi pose in vita sì dolce e soave
ch'io mi sentia dir dietro spesse fiate:
"Deo, per qual dignitate
così leggiadro questi lo core have?"

Or ho perduta tutta mia baldanza,
che si movea d'amoroso tesoro;
ond'io pover dimoro,
in guisa che di dir mi ven dottanza.
Sì che volendo far come coloro
che per vergogna celan lor mancanza,
di fuor mostro allegranza,
e dentro de lo core struggo e ploro.

This sonnet has two main parts. In the first I mean to call upon Love's faithful with the words of the prophet Jeremiah: *O vos omnes qui transitis per viam, attendite et videte si est dolor sicut dolor meus,*[7] and to beg that they deign to hear me; in the second part I tell of the condition in which Love had placed me, with a meaning other than that contained in the beginning and the ending of the sonnet, and I tell what I have lost. The second part begins: *Love—surely not.*

VIII

After the departure of this gentlewoman it pleased the Lord of the angels to call to His glory a young and very beautiful lady, who was known in the aforementioned city for her exceeding charm. I saw her body without the soul, lying in the midst of many ladies who were weeping most pitifully; then, remembering that I had seen her several times in the company of that most gracious one, I could not hold back my tears and, weeping, I resolved to say something about her death, in recognition of having seen her several times in the company of my lady. (And I suggest something of this toward the end of the words I wrote about her, as will be evident to the discerning reader.) I composed, then, these two sonnets, the first beginning: *If Love himself*, and the second: *Villainous death.*

If Love himself weep, shall not lovers weep,
  learning for what sad cause he pours his tears?
Love hears his ladies crying their distress,
  showing forth bitter sorrow through their eyes
  because villainous Death has worked its cruel

7. "All ye that pass by behold and see if there be any sorrow like unto my sorrow."

destructive art upon a gentle heart,
and laid waste all that earth can find to praise
in a gracious lady, save her chastity.

Hear then how Love paid homage to this lady:
I saw him weeping there in human form,
observing the stilled image of her grace;
and more than once he raised his eyes toward Heaven,
where that sweet soul already had its home,
which once, on earth, had worn enchanting flesh.

Piangete, amanti, poi che piange Amore,
udendo qual cagion lui fa plorare.
Amor sente a Pietà donne chiamare,
mostrando amaro duol per li occhi fore,
perché villana Morte in gentil core
ha miso il suo crudele adoperare,
guastando ciò che al mondo è da laudare
in gentil donna, sovra de l'onore.

Audite quanto Amor le fece orranza,
ch'io 'l vidi lamentare in forma vera
sovra la morta imagine avvenente;
e riguardava ver lo ciel sovente,
ove l'alma gentil già locata era,
che donna fu di sì gaia sembianza.

This sonnet is divided into three parts. In the first part I call
upon Love's faithful, imploring them to weep, and I say that
their lord himself weeps and that they, learning the reason for
his tears, should be more disposed to hear me. In the second part
I give the reason. In the third part I speak of a certain honor
that Love bestowed upon this lady. The second part begins:
learning for what, the third: *Hear then how.*

Villainous Death, at war with tenderness,
timeless mother of woe,
judgment severe and incontestable,

source of sick grief within my heart—a grief
    I constantly must bear—
    my tongue wears itself out in cursing you!
And if I want to make you beg for mercy,
    I need only reveal
    your felonies, your guilt of every guilt;
not that you are unknown for what you are,
    but rather to enrage
    whoever hopes for sustenance in love.

You have bereft the world of gentlest grace,
    of all that in sweet ladies merits praise;
    in youth's gay tender years
    you have destroyed all love's lightheartedness.
There is no need to name this gracious lady,
    because her qualities tell who she was.
    Who merits not salvation,
    let him not hope to share her company.

Morte villana, di pietà nemica,
    di dolor madre antica,
    giudicio incontastabile gravoso,
    poi che hai data matera al cor doglioso
    ond'io vado pensoso,
    di te blasmar la lingua s'affatica.
E s'io di grazia ti voi far mendica,
    convenesi ch'eo dica
    lo tuo fallar d'onni torto tortoso,
    non però ch'a la gente sia nascoso,
    ma per farne cruccioso
    chi d'amor per innanzi si notrica.

Dal secolo hai partita cortesia
    e ciò ch'è in donna da pregiar vertute:
    in gaia gioventute
    distrutta hai l'amorosa leggiadria.
Più non voi discovrir qual donna sia
    che per le proprietà sue canosciute.
    Chi non merta salute
    non speri mai d'aver sua compagnia.

The New Life

This sonnet is divided into four parts. In the first part I address Death with certain names appropriate to it; in the second I tell it why I curse it; in the third I revile it; in the fourth I allude to some unspecified person who, yet, is very clear to my mind. The second part begins: *source of sick grief,* the third: *And if I want,* the fourth: *Who merits not.*

IX

                Not long after the death of this lady something happened that made it necessary for me to leave the aforementioned city and go in the direction of (but not all the way to) the place where the lady who had formerly served as my screen was now staying. Though I was in the company of many others it was as if I were alone: the journey so irked me, because I was going farther away from my bliss, that my sighs could not relieve the anguish in my heart. Therefore his very sweet lordship, who ruled over me through the power of that most gracious lady, took the shape in my mind of a pilgrim scantily and poorly dressed. He seemed distressed; he stared continually at the ground except for the times his eyes seemed to turn toward a beautiful river, swift and very clear, flowing by the side of the road I was traveling. It seemed that Love called me and spoke these words: "I come from that lady who has been your shield for so long a time; I know that she will not return soon to your city, and so, that heart which I made you leave with her I now have with me, and I am carrying it to a lady who will now be your defense, just as the other lady was." He named her, and she was a lady I knew well. "If you should, however, repeat any of the things I have told you, do so in a way that will not reveal the insincerity of the love you showed for the first lady, and which you must now show for another." Having said these words, his image suddenly vanished from my mind, because Love had become so great a part of me; and as if transformed in my appearance, I rode on that day deep in thought, with my sighs for company. The next day I began writing a sonnet about all this, which begins: *As I rode out.*

As I rode out one day not long ago,
  by narrow roads, and heavy with the thought
  of what compelled my going, I met Love
  in pilgrim's rags, coming the other way.
All his appearance told the shabby story
  of a once-great ruler since bereft of power;
  and ever sighing, bent with thought, he moved,
  his eyes averted from the passers-by.

But he saw me and called me by my name,
  and said: "I come from that place far away
  where I had sent your heart to serve my will;
  I bring it back to court a new delight."
Then he began to fuse with me so strangely,
  he disappeared before I knew he had.

Cavalcando l'altrier per un cammino,
  pensoso de l'andar che mi sgradia,
  trovai Amore in mezzo de la via
  in abito leggier di peregrino.
Ne la sembianza mi parea meschino,
  come avesse perduto segnoria;
  e sospirando pensoso venia,
  per non veder la gente, a capo chino.

Quando mi vide, mi chiamò per nome,
  e disse: "Io vegno di lontana parte,
  ov'era lo tuo cor per mio volere;
  e recolo a servir novo piacere."
Allora presi di lui sì gran parte,
  ch'elli disparve, e non m'accorsi come.

This sonnet has three parts. In the first part I tell how I encountered Love and how he looked; in the second I relate what he told me—only in part, however, for fear of revealing my secret; in the third part I tell how he disappeared from me. The second part begins: *But he saw me,* the third: *Then he began.*

X

After returning from my journey I sought out that lady whom my lord had named to me on the road of sighs, and, to be brief, I shall say that in a short time I made her so completely my defense that many people commented on it more than courtesy would have permitted; this often caused me grave concern. And for this reason, that is, the exaggerated rumors which made me out to be a vicious person, my most gracious lady, scourge of all vices and queen of the virtues, passing along a certain way, denied me her most sweet greeting in which lay all my bliss. Now I should like to depart a little from the present subject in order to make clear the miraculous effect her greeting had on me.

XI

I must tell you that whenever and wherever she appeared, I, in anticipation of her miraculous greeting, could not have considered any man my enemy; on the contrary, a flame of charity was lit within me and made me forgive whoever had offended me. And if, at this moment, anyone had asked me about anything, I could only have answered, my face all kindness: "Love." And when she was about to greet me, one of Love's spirits, annihilating all the others of the senses, would drive out the feeble spirits of sight, saying to them, "Go and pay homage to your mistress," and Love would take their place. And if anyone had wished to know Love, he might have done so by looking at my glistening eyes. And when this most gracious one greeted me, Love was no medium capable of tempering my unbearable bliss, but rather, as if possessed of an excess of sweetness, he became so powerful that my body, which was completely under his rule, often moved like a heavy, inanimate object. By now it should be most evident that in her salutation dwelt my bliss, a bliss which often exceeded my capacity to contain it.

XII

Now, returning to my subject, let me say that no sooner was my bliss denied me than I was so stricken with anguish that, withdrawing from all company, I went to a solitary place to bathe the earth with bitterest tears. After my sobbing had quieted down somewhat, I went to my bedroom where I could lament without being heard; and there, begging pity of the lady of courtesy, and saying, "Love, help your faithful one," I fell asleep like a little boy crying from a spanking. About half-way through my sleep I seemed to see in my room a young man sitting near the bed dressed in the whitest of garments and, from his expression, he seemed to be deep in thought, watching me where I lay; after looking at me for some time, he seemed to sigh and to call to me, saying these words: *Fili mi, tempus est ut pretermictantur simulacra nostra.*[8] Then I seemed to know who he was, for he was calling me in the same way that many times before in my sleep he had called me; and as I watched him, it seemed to me that he was weeping piteously, and he seemed to be waiting for me to say something to him; so, gathering courage, I began to address him, saying: "Lord of all virtues, why do you weep?" And he said these words to

8. "My son, it is time to do away with our false ideals."

me: *Ego tanquam centrum circuli, cui simili modo se habent circumferentie partes; tu autem non sic.*[9] Then, as I thought over his words, it seemed to me that he had spoken very obscurely, so that I decided, reluctantly, to speak, and I said these words to him: "Why is it, my Lord, that you speak so obscurely?" And this time he spoke in Italian, saying: "Do not ask more than is useful to you." And so, I began telling him about the greeting that had been denied me, and when I asked him for the reason why, he answered me in this way: "Our Beatrice heard from certain people who were talking about you that your attentions to the lady I named to you on the road of sighs were doing her some harm; this is the reason why the most gracious one, who is the opposite of anything harmful, did not deign to greet you, fearing your person might prove harmful to her. Since she has really been more or less aware of your secret for quite some time, I want you to write a certain poem, in which you make clear the power I have over you through her, explaining that ever since you were a boy you have belonged to her; and, concerning this, call as witness him who knows, and say that you are begging him to testify on your behalf; and I, who am that witness, will gladly explain it to her, and from this she will understand your true feelings and, understanding them, she will also set the proper value on the words of those people who were mistaken. Let your words themselves be, as it were, an intermediary, whereby you will not be speaking directly to her, for this would not be fitting; and unless these words are accompanied by me, do not send them anywhere she could hear them; also be sure to adorn them with sweet music where I shall be present whenever this is necessary." Having said these words he disappeared, and my sleep was broken. Then I, thinking back, discovered that this vision had appeared to me during the ninth hour of the day;

9. "I am like the center of a circle, equidistant from all points on the circumference; you, however, are not."

before I left my room I decided to write a ballad following the instructions that my Lord had given me, and later on I composed this ballad which begins: *I want you to go, ballad.*

I want you to go, ballad, to seek out Love
    and present yourself with him before my lady,
    so that my exculpation, which you sing
    may be explained to her by Love, my lord.

Ballad, you move along so gracefully,
    you need no company
    to venture boldly anywhere you like,
    but if you want to go with full assurance,
    first make a friend of Love;
    perhaps to go alone would not be wise,
    because the lady you are meant to speak to
    is angry with me now (or so I think),
    and if you were to go your way without him,
    she might, perhaps, refuse to take you in.

But sweetly singing, in Love's company,
    start with these words (but only
    after you have begged her for compassion):
    "My lady, the one who sends me here to you
    hopes it will be your pleasure
    to hear me out and judge if he is guilty.
    I come with Love who, through your beauty's power,
    can make your lover's whole appearance change;
    now can you see why Love made him look elsewhere?
    Remember, though, his heart has never strayed."

And say to her: "That heart of his, my lady,
    has been so firmly faithful
    that every thought keeps him a slave to you;
    it was early yours, and never changed allegiance."
    If she should not believe you,
    tell her to question Love, who knows the truth;
    and end by offering this humble prayer:
    if granting me forgiveness would offend her,
    then may her answer sentence me to death,
    and she will see a faithful slave's obedience.

The New Life

And tell Love, who is all compassion's key,
   before you take your leave,
   tell Love, who will know how to plead my case,
thanks to the strains of my sweet melody:
   "Stay here awhile with her,
   talk to her of your servant as you will;
   and if your prayer should win for him reprieve,
let her clear smile announce that peace is made."
My gracious ballad, when it please you, go,
win yourself honor when the time is ripe.

Ballata, i' voi che tu ritrovi Amore,
   e con lui vade a madonna davante,
   sì che la scusa mia, la qual tu cante,
   ragioni poi con lei lo mio segnore.

Tu vai, ballata, sì cortesemente,
   che sanza compagnia
   dovresti avere in tutte parti ardire;
   ma se tu vuoli andar sicuramente,
   retrova l'Amor pria,
   ché forse non è bon sanza lui gire;
   però che quella che ti dée audire,
   sì com'io credo, è ver di me adirata:
   se tu di lui non fossi accompagnata,
   leggeramente ti faria disnore.

Con dolze sono, quando se' con lui,
   comincia este parole,
   appresso che averai chesta pietate:
   "Madonna, quelli che mi manda a vui,
   quando vi piaccia, vole,
   sed elli ha scusa, che la m'intendiate.
   Amore è qui, che per vostra bieltate
   lo face, come vol, vista cangiare:
   dunque perché li fece altra guardare
   pensatel voi, da che non mutò 'l core."

Dille: "Madonna, lo suo core è stato
   con sì fermata fede,

che 'n voi servir l'ha 'mpronto onne pensero:
tosto fu vostro, e mai non s'è smagato."
Sed ella non ti crede,
di' che domandi Amor, che sa lo vero:
ed a la fine falle umil preghero,
lo perdonare se le fosse a noia,
che mi comandi per messo ch'eo moia,
e vedrassi ubidir ben servidore.

E di' a colui ch'è d'ogni pietà chiave,
avante che sdonnei,
che le saprà contar mia ragion bona,
per grazia de la mia nota soave:
"Reman tu qui con lei,
e del tuo servo ciò che vuoi ragiona;
e s'ella per tuo prego li perdona,
fa che li annunzi un bel sembiante pace."
Gentil ballata mia, quando ti piace,
movi in quel punto che tu n'aggie onore.

This ballad is divided into three parts. In the first I tell it
where to go and encourage it so that it will go with more assurance, and I tell it whom it should have for company if it wishes
to go securely and free from any danger; in the second I tell
it what it is supposed to make known; in the third I give it per-
mission to depart whenever it pleases, commending its journey
to the arms of fortune. The second part begins: *But sweetly
singing*, the third: *My gracious ballad*.

Here one might make the objection that no one can know to
whom my words in the second person are addressed, since the
ballad is nothing more than the words I myself speak; and so
let me say that I intend to explain and discuss this uncertainty
in an even more difficult section of this little book; and if
anyone may have been in doubt here, perhaps wishing to offer
the objection mentioned above, let him understand, there, the
explanation to apply here as well.

XIII

After this last vision, when I had already written what Love commanded me to write, many and diverse thoughts began to assail and try me, against which I was defenseless; among these thoughts were four that seemed to disturb most my peace of mind. The first was this: the lordship of Love is good since he keeps the mind of his faithful servant away from all evil things. The next was this: the lordship of Love is not good because the more fidelity his faithful one shows him, the heavier and more painful are the moments he must live through. Another was this: the name of Love is so sweet to hear that it seems impossible to me that the effect itself should be in most things other than sweet, since, as has often been said, names are the consequences of the things they name: *Nomina sunt consequentia rerum*. The fourth was this: the lady through whom Love makes you suffer so is not like other ladies, whose hearts can be easily moved to change their attitudes.

And each one of these thoughts attacked me so forcefully that it made me feel like one who does not know what direction to take, who wants to start and does not know which way to go. And as for the idea of trying to find a common road for all of them, that is, one where all might come together, this was completely alien to me: namely, appealing to Pity and throwing myself into her arms. While I was in this mood, the desire to write some poetry about it came to me, and so I wrote this sonnet which begins: *All my thoughts*.

All my thoughts speak to me concerning Love;
    they have in them such great diversity
    that one thought makes me welcome all Love's power,
    another judges such a lordship folly,
    another, with its hope, brings me delight,

another very often makes me weep;
only in craving pity all agree
as they tremble with the fear that grips my heart.

I do not know from which to take my theme;
I want to speak, but what is there to say?
Thus do I wander in a maze of Love!
And if I want to harmonize them all,
I am forced to call upon my enemy,
Lady Pity, to come to my defense.

Tutti li miei penser parlan d'Amore;
a hanno in lor sì gran varietate,
ch'altro mi fa voler sua potestate,
altro folle ragiona il suo valore,
altro sperando m'apporta dolzore,
altro pianger mi fa spesse fiate;
e sol s'accordano in cherer pietate,
tremando di paura che è nel core.

Ond'io non so da qual matera prenda;
e vorrei dire, e non so ch'io mi dica.
Così mi trovo in amorosa erranza!
E se con tutti voi fare accordanza,
convenemi chiamar la mia nemica,
madonna la Pietà, che mi difenda.

This sonnet can be divided into four parts. In the first I say
and submit that all my thoughts are about Love; in the second
I say that they are different, and I talk about their differences;
in the third I tell what they all seem to have in common; in the
fourth I say that, wishing to speak of Love, I do not know
where to begin, and if I wish to take my theme from all my
thoughts, I would be forced to call upon my enemy, my Lady
Pity—and I use the term "my lady" rather scornfully. The
second part begins: *they have in them;* the third: *only in*
craving; the fourth: *I do not know.*

The New Life   23

After the battle of the conflicting thoughts it happened that my most gracious lady was present where many gentlewomen were gathered. I was taken there by a friend who thought I would be delighted to go to a place where so many beautiful ladies were. I was not sure why I was being taken there but, trusting in the person who had led his friend to the threshold of death, I asked him: "Why have we come to see these ladies?" He answered: "So that they may be fittingly attended." The fact is that they were gathered there to be with a certain lovely lady who had been married that day, for according to the custom of the afore-mentioned city they were supposed to keep her company during the first meal at the home of her bridegroom. So I, thinking to please my friend, decided to remain with him in attendance upon the ladies. No sooner had I reached this decision than I seemed to feel a strange throbbing which began in the left side of my breast and immediately spread to all parts of my body. Then, pretending to act naturally, I leaned for support against a painted surface that extended along the walls of the house and, fearing that people might have become aware of my trembling, I raised my eyes and, looking at the ladies, I saw among them the most gracious Beatrice. Then my spirits were so disrupted by the strength Love acquired when he saw himself this close to the most gracious lady, that none survived except the spirits of sight; and even these were driven forth, because Love desired to occupy their enviable post in order to behold the marvelous lady. And even though I was not quite myself, I was still very sorry for these little spirits who bitterly protested, saying: "If this one had not thrust us from our place like a bolt of lightning, we could have stayed to see the wonders of this lady as all our peers are doing." Now many of the ladies present, noticing the transformation I had undergone, were amazed and began to talk about it, joking about me with that most gracious one. My friend, who had made a mistake in good faith, took me by the hand and, leading me out of the sight of the ladies, asked me what was wrong. Then I, somewhat restored, for my dead spirits were coming back to life, and the ones ejected were returning to their rightful domain, said these words to my friend: "I have just set foot on that boundary of life beyond which no one can go, hoping to return." And leaving him, I went back to my room of tears where, weeping in humiliation, I said to myself: "If this lady were aware of my condition, I do not believe she would ridicule my appearance but, on the contrary, would feel pity." In the midst of my tears I thought of writing a few words addressed to her, explaining the reason for the change in my appearance and saying that I was well aware that no one knew the reason and that, if it were known, I believed it would arouse everyone's compassion; I decided to write this in the hope that my words by chance would reach her. Then I composed this sonnet which begins: *You join with other ladies.*

You join with other ladies to make sport
    of the way I look, my lady, and do not ask
    what makes me cut so laughable a figure
    when I am in the presence of your beauty.
    If only you knew why, I am sure that Pity
    would drop her arms and make her peace with me;
    for Love, when he discovers me near you,
    takes on a cruel, bold new confidence

and puts my frightened senses to the sword,
    by slaying this one, driving that one out,
    till only he is left to look at you.
    Thus, by the changeling Love, I have been changed,
    but not so much that I cannot still hear
    my outcast senses mourning in their pain.

Con l'altre donne mia vista gabbate,
  e non pensate, donna, onde si mova
  ch'io vi rassembri sì figura nova
  quando riguardo la vostra beltate.
  Se lo saveste, non poria Pietate
  tener più contra me l'usata prova,
  ché Amor, quando sì presso a voi mi trova,
  prende baldanza e tanta securtate,

che fere tra' miei spiriti paurosi,
  e quale ancide, e qual pinge di fore,
  sì che solo remane a veder vui.
  Ond'io mi cangio in figura d'altrui,
  ma non sì ch'io non senta bene allore
  li guai de li scacciati tormentosi.

I do not divide this sonnet into parts, since this is done only to help reveal the meaning of the thing divided; and since what has been said about its occasion is sufficiently clear, there is no need for division. True, among the words with which I relate the occasion for this sonnet, there occur certain expressions difficult to understand, as when I say that Love slays all my spirits and the spirits of sight remain alive, though driven outside their organs. But it is impossible to make this clear to anyone who is not as faithful a follower of Love as I; to those who are, the solution to the difficulty is already obvious. Therefore, there is no need for me to clear up such difficulties, for my words of clarification would be either meaningless or superfluous.

XV

After that strange transformation a certain thought began to oppress my mind; it seldom left me but rather continually nagged at me, and it took form in this way: "Since you become so ridiculous-looking whenever you are near this lady, why do you keep trying to see her? Now assume that she were to ask you this, and that all your faculties were free to answer her, what would your answer be?" And to this another thought replied, saying modestly, "If I did not lose my wits and felt able to answer her, I would tell her that as soon as I call to mind the miraculous image of her beauty, then the desire to see her overcomes me, a desire so powerful that it kills, it destroys anything in my memory that might have been able to restrain it; and that is why what I have suffered in the past does not keep me from trying to see her." Moved by such thoughts, I decided to write a few words in which I would acquit myself of the accusation suggested by the first thought, and also describe what happens to me whenever I am near her. Then I wrote this sonnet which begins: *Whatever might restrain me.*

> Whatever might restrain me when I feel drawn
>   to see you, my heart's bliss, dies from my mind.
>   When I come close to you, I hear Love's warning:
>   "Unless you want to die, run away now!"
> My blanching face reveals my fainting heart
>   which weakly seeks support from where it may,
>   and as I tremble in this drunken state
>   the stones in the wall I lean on shout back: "Die!"
>
> He sins who witnesses my transformation
>   and will not comfort my tormented soul,
>   at least by showing that he shares my grief
> for pity's sake—which by your mocking dies,
>   once it is brought to life by my dying face,
>   whose yearning eyes beg death to take me now.

> *Ciò che m'incontra, ne la mente more,*
>   *quand'i' vegno a veder voi, bella gioia.*
>   *E quand'io vi son presso, i' sento Amore*
>   *che dice: "Fuggi, se 'l perir t'è noia."*
> *Lo viso mostra lo color del core,*
>   *che, tramortendo, ovunque pò s'appoia,*

The New Life

e per la ebrietà del gran tremore
le pietre par che gridin: "Moia, moia."

Peccato face chi allora mi vide,
se l'alma sbigottita non conforta,
sol dimostrando che di me li doglia,
per la pietà, che 'l vostro gabbo ancide,
la qual si cria ne la vista morta
de li occhi, c'hanno di lor morte voglia.

This sonnet is divided into two parts. In the first I explain why I do not keep myself from seeking this lady's company; in the second I tell what happens to me when I go near her, and this part begins: *When I come close.* This second part can be further divided into five sections, according to five different themes. In the first I tell what Love, counseled by reason, says to me whenever I am near her; in the second I describe the condition of my heart by reference to my face; in the third I tell how all assurance grows faint in me; in the fourth I say that he sins who does not show pity, which might be of some comfort to me; in the last part I tell why others should have pity, namely, because of the piteous look which fills my eyes. But this piteous look is wasted; it is never really seen by anyone, all because of the mockery of this lady who causes others, who perhaps might have noticed this piteousness, to do as she does. The second part begins: *My blanching face;* the third: *and as I tremble;* the fourth: *He sins;* the fifth: *for pity's sake.*

XVI

Soon after completing this sonnet I was moved by a desire to write more poetry, in which I would mention four more things concerning my condition which, it seemed to me, I had not yet made clear. The first of these is that many times I suffered when my memory excited my imagination to re-evoke the transformations that Love worked in me. The second is that Love, frequently and without warning, attacked me so violently that no part of me remained alive except one thought that spoke of this lady. The third is that when this battle of Love raged within me so, I would go, pale and haggard, to look upon this lady, believing that the sight of her would defend me in this battle, forgetting what happened to me whenever I approached such graciousness. The fourth is that not only did the sight of her not defend me: it ultimately annihilated the little life I had left. And so I wrote this sonnet which begins: *Time and again.*

> Time and again the thought comes to my mind
>   of the dark condition Love imparts to me;
>   then the pity of it strikes me, and I ask:
>   "Could ever anyone have felt the same?"
>   For Love's attack is so precipitous
>   that life itself all but abandons me:
>   nothing survives except one lonely spirit,
>   allowed to live because it speaks of you.
>
> With hope of help to come I gather courage,
>   and deathly languid, drained of all defenses,
>   I come to you expecting to be healed;
>   and if I raise my eyes to look at you,
>   within my heart a tremor starts to spread,
>   driving out life, stopping my pulses' beat.

> *Spesse fiate vegnonmi a la mente*
>   *le oscure qualità ch'Amor mi dona,*
>   *e vermene pietà, sì che sovente*
>   *io dico: "Lasso!, avviene elli a persona?"*
>   *ch'Amor m'assale subitanamente,*
>   *sì che la vita quasi m'abbandona:*
>   *campami un spirto vivo solamente,*
>   *e que' riman perché di voi ragiona.*
>
> *Poscia mi sforzo, ché mi voglio atare;*
>   *e così smorto, d'onne valor voto,*

vegno a vedervi, credendo guerire;
e se io levo li occhi per guardare,
nel cor mi si comincia uno tremoto,
che fa de' polsi l'anima partire.

This sonnet is divided into four parts according to the four things it treats, and since these are explained above, I concern myself only with indicating the parts by their beginnings; accordingly, the second part begins: *For Love's attack;* the third: *With hope of help;* the fourth: *and if I raise.*

XVII

After I had written these three sonnets addressed to this lady, in which little concerning my condition was left unsaid, believing I should be silent and say no more about this even at the cost of never again writing to her, since it seemed to me that I had talked about myself enough, I felt forced to find a new theme, one nobler than the last. Because I think the occasion for my new theme is a story pleasant to hear, I shall tell it, and as briefly as possible.

XVIII

Because of my appearance many people had learned the secret of my heart, and certain ladies who had seen me swoon at one time or another, and who knew my heart very well, happened to be gathered together one day, enjoying each other's company, when I, as if guided by fortune, passed near them and heard one of these gentlewomen call to me. The lady who addressed me had a very lively way of speaking, and so, when I had come up to them and saw that my most gracious lady was not with them, gaining confidence, I greeted them and asked what I could do to please them. There were many ladies present: several were laughing together; others were looking at me as if waiting for me to say something; there were others talking among themselves—one of whom, turning her eyes toward me and calling me by name, said: "Why do you love this lady of yours, if you are unable to endure the sight of her? Tell us, for surely the goal of such a love must be strange indeed." After she had said these words, not only she but all the others showed by their expression that they were waiting for my answer. I said: "Ladies, the goal of my love once consisted in receiving the greeting of this lady to whom you are, perhaps, referring, and in this greeting rested the bliss which was the goal of all my desires. But since it pleased her to deny it to me, my lord, Love, through his grace, has placed all my bliss in something that cannot fail me." With this the ladies began to speak among themselves and, just as sometimes the rain can be seen falling mingled with beautiful flakes of snow, so did I seem to hear their words issuing forth mingled with sighs. After they had spoken to each other for awhile, the one who had first addressed me spoke to me again, saying: "We beg you to tell us where this bliss of yours now rests." And I answered her: "In those words that praise my lady." And the one who had asked me the question said: "If you are telling us the truth, then those words you addressed to her describing your condition must have been written with some other intention." Then I, shamed by her words, departed from these ladies, saying to myself: "Since there is so much bliss in words that praise my lady, why have I ever written in any other way?" Therefore, I resolved that from then on I would always choose as the theme of my poetry whatever would be in praise of this most gracious one. Then, reflecting more on this, it seemed to me that I had undertaken a theme too lofty for myself, so that I did not dare to begin writing, and I remained for several days with the desire to write and the fear of beginning.

XIX

Then it happened that while walking down a path along which ran a very clear stream, I suddenly felt a great desire to write a poem, and I began to think how I would go about it. It seemed to me that to speak of my lady would not be becoming unless I were to address my words to ladies, and not just to any ladies, but only to those who are worthy, not merely to women. Then, I must tell you, my tongue, as if moved of its own accord, spoke and said: *Ladies who have intelligence of love*. With great delight I decided to keep these words in mind and to use them as the beginning of my poem. Later, after returning to the aforementioned city and reflecting for several days, I began writing a *canzone*, using this beginning, and I constructed it in a way that will appear below in its divisions. The *canzone* begins: *Ladies who have*.

Ladies who have intelligence of love,
   I wish to speak to you about my lady,
   not thinking to complete her litany,
   but to talk in order to relieve my heart.
   I tell you, when I think of her perfection,
   Love lets me feel the sweetness of his presence,
   and if at that point I could still feel bold,
   my words could make all mankind fall in love.
   I do not want to choose a tone too lofty,
   for fear that such ambition make me timid;
   instead I shall discuss her graciousness,
   defectively, to measure by her merit,
   with you, ladies and maidens whom Love knows,
   for such a theme is only fit for you.

The mind of God receives an angel's prayer:
   "My Lord, there appears to be upon your earth
   a living miracle, proceeding from
   a radiant soul whose light reaches us here."

Heaven, that lacks its full perfection only
in lacking her, pleads for her to the Lord,
and every saint is begging for this favor.
Compassion for His creatures still remains,
for God, who knows they are speaking of my lady,
says: "Chosen ones, now suffer happily
that she, your hope, live her appointed time
for the sake of one down there who fears her loss,
and who shall say unto the damned in Hell:
'I have beheld the hope of Heaven's blest.' "

My lady is desired in highest Heaven.
    Now let me tell you something of her power.
    A lady who aspires to graciousness
    should seek her company, for where she goes
    Love drives a killing frost into vile hearts
    that freezes and destroys what they are thinking;
    should such a one insist on looking at her,
    he is changed to something noble or he dies.
    And if she finds one worthy to behold her,
    that man will feel her power for salvation
    when she accords to him her salutation,
    which humbles him till he forgets all wrongs.
    God has graced her with an even greater gift:
    whoever speaks with her shall speak with Him.

Love says of her: "How can a mortal body
    achieve such beauty and such purity?"
    He looks again and swears it must be true:
    God does have something new in mind for earth.
    Her color is the pallor of the pearl,
    a paleness perfect for a gracious lady;
    she is the best that Nature can achieve
    and by her mold all beauty tests itself;
    her eyes, wherever she may choose to look,
    send forth their spirits radiant with love
    to strike the eyes of anyone they meet,
    and penetrate until they find the heart.
    You will see Love depicted on her face,
    there where no one dares hold his gaze too long.

The New Life

My song, I know that you will go and speak
   to many ladies when I bid you leave,
   and since I brought you up as Love's true child,
   ingenuous and plain, let me advise you
   to beg of anybody you may meet:
   "Please help me find my way; I have been sent
   to the lady with whose praise I am adorned."
   And so that you may not have gone in vain,
   do not waste time with any vulgar people;
   do what you can to show your meaning only
   to ladies, or to men who may be worthy;
   they will direct you by the quickest path.
   You will find Love and with him find our lady.
   Speak well of me to Love, it is your duty.

Donne ch'avete intelletto d'amore,
   i' vo' con voi de la mia donna dire,
   non perch'io creda sua laude finire,
   ma ragionar per isfogar la mente.
   Io dico che pensando il suo valore,
   Amor sì dolce mi si fa sentire,
   che s'io allora non perdessi ardire,
   farei parlando innamorar la gente.
   E io non vo' parlar sì altamente,
   ch'io divenisse per temenza vile;
   ma tratterò del suo stato gentile
   a respetto di lei leggeramente,
   donne e donzelle amorose, con vui,
   ché non è cosa da parlarne altrui.

Angelo clama in divino intelletto
   e dice: "Sire, nel mondo si vede
   maraviglia ne l'atto che procede
   d'un'anima che 'nfin qua su risplende."
   Lo cielo, che non have altro difetto
   che d'aver lei, al suo segnor la chiede,
   e ciascun santo ne grida merzede.
   Sola Pietà nostra parte difende,
   che parla Dio, che di madonna intende:
   "Diletti miei, or sofferite in pace

           Dante's Vita Nuova

che vostra spene sia quanto me piace
là 'v'è alcun che perder lei s'attende,
e che dirà ne lo inferno: 'O mal nati,
io vidi la speranza de' beati.' "

Madonna è disiata in sommo cielo:
or voi di sua virtù farvi savere.
Dico, qual vuol gentil donna parere
vada con lei, che quando va per via,
gitta nei cor villani Amore un gelo,
per che onne lor pensero agghiaccia e pere;
e qual soffrisse di starla a vedere
diverria nobil cosa, o si morria.
E quando trova alcun che degno sia
di veder lei, quei prova sua vertute,
ché li avvien, ciò che li dona, in salute,
e sì l'umilia, ch'ogni offesa oblia.
Ancor l'ha Dio per maggior grazia dato
che non pò mal finir chi l'ha parlato.

Dice di lei Amor: "Cosa mortale
come esser pò sì adorna e sì pura?"
Poi la reguarda, e fra se stesso giura
che Dio ne 'ntenda di far cosa nova.
Color di perle ha quasi, in forma quale
convene a donna aver, non for misura;
ella è quanto de ben pò far natura;
per essemplo di lei bieltà si prova.
De li occhi suoi, come ch'ella li mova,
escono spirti d'amore infiammati,
che feron li occhi a qual che allor la guati,
e passan sì che' l cor ciascun retrova:
voi le vedete Amor pinto nel viso,
là 've non pote alcun mirarla fiso.

Canzone, io so che tu girai parlando
a donne assai, quand'io t'avrò avanzata.
Or t'ammonisco, perch'io t'ho allevata
per figliuola d'Amor giovane e piana,
che là 've giugni tu diche pregando:
"Insegnatemi gir, ch'io son mandata

The New Life

35

> *a quella di cui laude so' adornata."*
> *E se non vuoli andar sì come vana,*
> *non restare ove sia gente villana:*
> *ingegnati, se puoi, d'esser palese*
> *solo con donne o con omo cortese,*
> *che ti merranno là per via tostana.*
> *Tu troverai Amor con esso lei;*
> *reccomandami a lui come tu dei.*

In order that this *canzone* may be better understood I shall divide it more carefully than the previous poems. I first divide it into three parts: the first part is an introduction to the words that follow; the second continues the theme treated; the third is, as it were, a servant to the words that precede it. The second part begins: *The mind of God*, the third: *My song, I know.* Now the first part falls into four subdivisions. In the first I tell to whom I wish to write; in the second I tell about the condition in which I find myself whenever I think of her perfection, and how I would write if I did not lose courage; in the third I mention the way in which I intend to write about her in order not to be intimidated; in the fourth, referring again to those to whom I mean to write, I give the reason why I have chosen them. The second begins: *I tell you;* the third: *I do not want;* the fourth: *with you, ladies.*

Then, when I say: *The mind of God,* I begin to talk about my lady, and this part falls into two subdivisions. In the first I tell how she is thought of in Heaven; in the second I tell how she is thought of on earth: *My lady is desired.* This second part, in turn, is divided into two. In the first I describe the nobility of her soul, telling about the effective powers that proceed from it; in the second I describe the nobility of her body, telling about some of its beautiful qualities: *Love says of her.* The second part is in turn divided into two. In the first I speak of certain beautiful qualities involving particular parts of her body: *her eyes, wherever.* This is again divided in two. First I speak of her eyes, which are the initiators of love; then I speak of her mouth, which is the supreme desire of my love. So that here and now any perverse thought may be dispelled, let him who reads this remember what has been previously said about this lady's greeting, which was an action of her mouth, and which was the goal of all my desires so long as I was allowed to receive it.

Then when I say, *My song, I know that you,* I am adding a stanza as a sort of handmaiden to the others. In this stanza I tell what I want my song to do; because this last part is easy to understand, I do not bother to divide it further. Certainly, to make the meaning of this *canzone* still clearer, I should have to make the divisions even more minute; however, if anyone is not intelligent enough to understand it from the divisions already made, I would not mind in the least if he would simply leave my poem alone. As it is, I am afraid I may have shared its meaning with too many readers because of these divisions I have already made—if it should happen that many would bother to read them.

XX

After this *canzone* had become rather well known, one of my friends who had heard it was moved to ask me to write about the nature of Love, having perhaps, from reading my poem, acquired more confidence in me than I deserved. So, thinking that after my treatment of the previous theme it would be good to treat the theme of Love and, feeling that I owed this to my friend, I decided to compose a poem dealing with Love. And I wrote this sonnet, which begins: *Love and the gracious heart.*

Love and the gracious heart are a single thing,
    as Guinizelli tells us in his poem:

The New Life

one can no more be without the other
than can the reasoning mind without its reason.
Nature, when in a loving mood, creates them:
Love to be king, the heart to be his home,
a place for Love to rest while he is sleeping,
perhaps for just a while, or for much longer.

And then the beauty of a virtuous lady
appears, to please the eyes, and in the heart
desire for the pleasing thing is born;
and this desire may linger in the heart
until Love's spirit is aroused from sleep.
A man of worth has the same effect on ladies.

Amore e 'l cor gentil sono una cosa,
sì come il saggio in suo dittare pone
e così esser l'una sanza l'altro osa
com'alma razional sanza ragione.
Falli natura quand'è amorosa,
Amor per sire e 'l cor per sua magione,
dentro la qual dormendo si riposa
tal volta poca e tal lunga stagione.

Bieltate appare in saggia donna pui,
che piace a li occhi sì, che dentro al core
nasce un disio de la cosa piacente;
e tanto dura talora in costui,
che fa svegliar lo spirito d'Amore.
E simil face in donna omo valente.

This sonnet is divided into two parts. In the first I speak of
Love as a potential force; in the second I speak of him as
potentiality realized in action. The second part begins: *And
then the beauty*. The first part is again divided into two: first,
I tell in what kind of substance this potentiality resides; secondly, I tell how this substance and this potentiality are brought
into being, and how the one is related to the other as matter is
to form. The second subdivision begins: *Nature, when*. Then
when I say: *And then the beauty*, I explain how this potenti-

ality is realized in action: first, how it is realized in a man, then how it is realized in a lady, beginning: *A man of worth.*

XXI

After having dealt with Love in the last sonnet, I felt a desire to write more, this time in praise of that most gracious lady, showing how, through her, this Love is awakened, and how she not only awakens him there where he sleeps but also, how she, miraculously working, brings him into existence there where he does not potentially exist. And so I wrote this sonnet which begins: *The power of Love.*

The power of Love borne in my lady's eyes
    imparts its grace to all she looks upon.
    All turn to gaze at her when she walks by,
    and when she greets a man his heart beats fast,
    the color leaves his face, he bows his head
    and sighs to think of all his imperfections.
    Anger and pride are forced to flee from her.
    Help me to honor her, most gracious ladies.

Humility and every sweet conception
    bloom in the heart of those who hear her speak.
    (Praise to the one who first saw what she was!)
    The image of her when she starts to smile
    dissolves within the mind and melts away,
    a miracle too rich and strange to hold.

Ne li occhi porta la mia donna Amore,
    per che si fa gentil ciò ch'ella mira;
    ov'ella passa, ogn'om ver lei si gira,
    e cui saluta fa tremar lo core,
    sì che, bassando il viso, tutto smore,
    e d'ogni suo difetto allor sospira:
    fugge dinanzi a lei superbia ed ira.
    Aiutatemi, donne, farle onore.

Ogne dolcezza, ogne pensero umile
nasce nel core a chi parlar la sente,
ond'è laudato chi prima la vide.
Quel ch'ella par quando un poco sorride,
non si pò dicer né tenere a mente,
sì è novo miracolo e gentile.

This sonnet has three parts. In the first I tell how this lady actualizes this potentiality by means of her most gracious eyes; in the third I tell how she does the same by means of her most gracious mouth; and between these two parts is a very small part, which is like a beggar asking for help from the preceding and following parts, and it begins: *Help me to honor her.* The third begins: *Humility.* The first part divides into three. In the first I tell how she miraculously makes gracious whatever she looks upon, and this is as much as to say that she brings Love into potential existence there where he does not exist; in the second I tell how she activates Love in the hearts of all those whom she sees; in the third I tell of what she miraculously effects in their hearts. The second part begins: *Men turn to gaze,* and the third: *and when she greets.* Then when I say: *Help me to honor,* I indicate to whom I wish to speak, calling upon ladies for their assistance in honoring my lady. Then when I say: *Humility,* I repeat what I said in the first part, using, this time, two actions of her mouth: the first is her sweet manner of speaking, the second is her miraculous smile. I do not mention the effect of the latter on people's hearts, since the memory is not capable of retaining a smile like hers or its effects.

XXII

Not many days after this, according to the will of the Lord of Glory (who Himself accepted death), he who had been the father of such a miraculous being as this most gracious Beatrice clearly was, departed from this life, passing most certainly into eternal glory. Since such a departure is sorrowful to those who remain and who have been friends of the deceased; and since there is no friendship more intimate than that of a good father for a good child, or of a good child for a good father; and since this lady possessed the highest degree of goodness; and since her father, as is believed by many, and is the truth, was exceedingly good—then it is clear that this lady was filled with bitterest sorrow. And since it was the custom of this city for ladies to gather with ladies and men with men on such occasions, many ladies were assembled in that place where Beatrice wept piteously. I saw several of them returning from her house and heard them talking about this most gracious one and how she mourned; among their words I heard: "She grieves so that anyone who sees her would surely die of pity." Then these ladies passed by me, and I was left in such a sad state that tears kept running down my face so that I often had to cover my eyes with my hands. I would have hidden myself as soon as I felt the tears coming, but I hoped to hear more about her, since I was standing where most of those ladies would pass by me after taking leave of her. And so, while I stayed in the same place, more ladies passed by me talking to each other, saying: "Who of us can ever be happy again after hearing this lady grieve so piteously?" After these, other ladies passed, saying as they came: "This man here is weeping exactly as if he had seen her, as we have." Then came others who said: "Look at him! He is so changed, he doesn't seem to be the same person." And so, as the ladies passed, I heard their words about her and about me, as I have just related. After reflecting awhile, I decided, since I had such an excellent theme, to write a poem in which I would include everything I had heard these ladies say. And since I would have been glad to question them, if I had not thought it would be indiscreet, I presented my theme as if I had asked them questions and they had answered me. I composed two sonnets: in the first I ask those questions which I had wanted to ask; in the other I give the ladies' answer, using what I had heard them say and presenting it as if they had said it in reply to me. The first sonnet begins: *O you who bear*, and the other: *Are you the one*.

> O you who bear a look of resignation,
>   moving with eyes downcast to show your grief,
>   where are you coming from? Your coloring
>   appears to be the hue of grief itself.
>   Is it our gracious lady you have seen
>   bathing with tears Love's image in her face?
>   O ladies, tell me what my heart tells me:
>   I see her grace in every step you take.
>
> And if you come from so profound a grief,
>   may it please you to stay with me awhile
>   and tell me truly what you know of her.
>   I see your eyes, I see how they have wept,
>   and how you come retreating all undone;
>   my heart is touched and shaken at the sight.

> *Voi che portate la sembianza umile,*
>   *con li occhi bassi, mostrando dolore,*
>   *onde venite che 'l vostro colore*
>   *par divenuto de pietà simile?*
>   *Vedeste voi nostra donna gentile*
>   *bagnar nel viso suo di pianto Amore?*
>   *Ditelmi, donne, che 'l mi dice il core,*
>   *perch'io vi veggio andar sanz'atto vile.*
>
> *E se venite da tanta pietate,*
>   *piacciavi di restar qui meco alquanto,*
>   *e qual che sia di lei, nol mi celate.*
>   *Io veggio li occhi vostri c'hanno pianto,*
>   *e veggiovi tornar sì sfigurate,*
>   *che 'l cor mi triema di vederne tanto.*

This sonnet divides into two parts. In the first I address these ladies and ask them if they come from my lady, telling them that I believe they do, since they come back as if made more gracious; in the second I ask them to talk to me about her. The second part begins: *And if you come.*

Here follows the other sonnet, composed in the way explained previously:

> Are you the one that often spoke to us
>   about our lady, and to us alone?
> Your tone of voice, indeed, resembles his,
> but in your face we find another look.
> Why do you weep so bitterly? Pity
> would melt the heart of anyone who sees you.
> Have you seen her weep, too, and now cannot
> conceal from us the sorrow in your heart?
>
> Leave grief to us; the path of tears is ours
>   (to try to comfort us would be a sin),
> we are the ones who heard her sobbing words.
> Her face proclaims the agony she feels;
> if anyone had dared look into her eyes,
> he would have died, drowned in his tears of grief.

> *Se' tu colui c'hai trattato sovente*
>   *di nostra donna, sol parlando a nui?*
> *Tu risomigli a la voce ben lui,*
>   *ma la figura ne par d'altra gente.*
> *E perché piangi tu sì coralmente,*
>   *che fai di te pietà venire altrui?*
> *Vedestù pianger lei, che tu non pui*
>   *punto celar la dolorosa mente?*
>
> *Lascia piangere noi e triste andare*
>   *(e fa peccato chi mai ne conforta),*
> *che nel suo pianto l'udimmo parlare.*
> *Ell'ha nel viso la pietà sì scorta,*
>   *che qual l'avesse voluta mirare*
> *sarebbe innanzi lei piangendo morta.*

This sonnet has four parts according to the four responses of the ladies for whom I speak, and since they are made evident enough in the sonnet, I do not bother to explain the meaning of the parts: I merely indicate where they occur. The second begins: *Why do you weep,* the third: *Leave grief to us,* the fourth: *Her face proclaims.*

XXIII

A few days after this it happened that my body was afflicted by a painful disease which made me suffer intense anguish continuously for nine days; I became so weak that I was forced to lie in bed like a person paralyzed. Now, on the ninth day, when the pain was almost unbearable, a thought came to me which was about my lady. After thinking about her awhile, I returned to thoughts of my feeble condition and, realizing how short life is, even if one is healthy, I began to weep silently about the misery of life. Then, sighing deeply, I said to myself: "It is bound to happen that one day the most gracious Beatrice will die." At that, such a frenzy seized me that I closed my eyes and, agitated like one in delirium, began to imagine things: as my mind started wandering, there appeared to me certain faces of ladies with dishevelled hair, and they were saying to me: "You are going to die." And then after these ladies there appeared to me other faces strange and horrible to look at, who were saying: "You are dead." While my imagination was wandering like this, I came to the point that I no longer knew where I was. And I seemed to see ladies preternaturally sad, their hair dishevelled, weeping as they made their way down a street. And I seemed to see the sun grow dark, giving the stars a color that would have made me swear that they were weeping. And it seemed to me that the birds flying through the air fell to earth dead, and there were violent earthquakes. Bewildered as I dreamed, and terrified, I imagined that a friend of mine came to tell me: "Then you don't know?

Your miraculous lady has departed from this world." At that I began to weep most piteously, and I wept not only in my dream, I wept with my eyes, wet with real tears. I imagined that I looked up at the sky, and I seemed to see a multitude of angels returning above, and they had before them a little pure-white cloud. It seemed to me that these angels were singing in glory, and the words of their song seemed to be: *Osanna in excelsis;*[10] the rest I could not seem to hear. Then it seemed that my heart, which was so full of love, said to me: "It is true, our lady lies dead." And hearing that, it seemed to me I went to see the body in which that most noble and blessed soul had dwelt, and in the intensity of my hallucination I saw this lady dead. And it seemed that ladies were covering her head with a white veil, and her face seemed to have an expression of such joyous acceptance that it said to me: "I am contemplating the fountainhead of peace." At the sight of her in this dream I felt such a serenity that I called upon Death and said: "Sweet Death, come to me. Do not be unkind to me: you should be gracious, considering where you have just been. So, come to me, for I earnestly desire you, and you can see that I do, for I already wear your color." And when I had witnessed the administering of the sorrowful rites customarily performed on the bodies of the dead, it seemed I returned to my room and from there looked toward Heaven, and so vivid was my dream that, weeping, I began to speak aloud: "O most beautiful soul, how blessed is he who beholds you!" As I was saying these words in a spasm of tears, calling upon Death to come to me, a young and gracious lady, who had been at my bedside, thought that my tears and words were caused by the pain of my illness, and greatly frightened began to weep. Then other ladies who were about the room became aware of my weeping because of her reaction to me. After sending away this lady, who was most

10. "Hosanna in the highest."

closely related to me, they drew near to wake me, thinking that I was having a dream, and said to me: "You must wake up" and "Do not be afraid." And with these words of theirs my wild imaginings were cut off just when I was about to say: "Oh, Beatrice, blessed art thou," and I had already said: "Oh, Beatrice," when I opened my eyes with a start and realized that it had been only a dream. Although I had called out this name, my voice was so broken by my sobbing that I think these ladies were not able to understand what I said. Even though I was very much ashamed, still, somehow prompted by Love, I turned my face toward them. And when they saw me, they began saying: "He looks as if he were dead!" And they said to each other: "Let us try to comfort him." And so they said many things to comfort me, and then they asked me what it was that had frightened me. Being somewhat comforted, aware that nothing was true of what I had imagined, I answered them: "I will tell you what happened to me." Then I began at the beginning and continued to the end, telling them what I had seen but without mentioning the name of the most gracious one.

After I had recovered from my illness, I decided to write about what had happened to me, since it seemed to me this would be something fascinating to hear about. And so I composed the *canzone* which begins: *A lady of tender years;* it is constructed in a manner made clear in the divisions that follow it.

> A lady of tender years, compassionate
>   and richly graced with human gentleness,
>   was standing near and heard me call on Death;
>   she saw the piteous weeping of my eyes
>   and heard the wild confusing words I spoke;
>   she was so struck with fear she wept aloud.
>   Then other ladies, made aware of me
>   by the weeping figure standing by my bed,
>   sent her away from there;

and they drew near to rouse me from my sleep.
One of them said: "Wake up!"
Another asked: "Why are you so distressed?"
With this I left my world of dreams and woke,
Calling aloud the name of my sweet lady.

I called to her in a voice so weak with pain,
   so broken by my tears and anguished sobs,
   that only my heart heard her name pronounced.
In spite of my deep-felt humiliation
   which showed itself most plainly on my face,
   Love made me turn and look up at these ladies.
The pallor of my skin amazed them so
   they could not help but start to speak of death.
"Oh, let us comfort him,"
   implored one lady sweetly of another;
   and more than once they asked:
"What did you see that took away your strength?"
When I felt comforted somewhat, I said:
"Ladies, now you shall know what I have seen:

While I was brooding on my languid life,
   and sensed how fleeting is our little day,
   Love wept within my heart, which is his home;
then my bewildered soul went numb with fear,
   and sighing deep within myself, I said:
   'My lady someday surely has to die.'
Then I surrendered to my anguished thoughts,
   and closed my heavy wept-out tired eyes,
   and all my body's spirits
   went drifting off, each fainting in despair.
And then, drifting and dreaming,
   with consciousness and truth left far behind,
   I saw the looks of ladies wild with wrath,
   chanting together: 'Die, you are going to die.'

Now captured by my false imaginings
   and somehow in a place unknown to me,
   I was the witness of unnatural things:
   of ladies passing with dishevelled hair,

The New Life

some weeping, others wailing their laments
that pierced the air like arrows tipped in flame.
And then it seemed to me I saw the sun
grow slowly darker, and a star appear,
and sun and star did weep;
birds flying through the air fell dead to earth;
the earth began to quake.
A man appeared, pale, and his voice was weak
as he said to me: 'You have not heard the news?
Your lady, once so lovely, now lies dead.'

I raised my weeping eyes to look above
and saw what seemed to be a rain of manna:
angels who were returning to their home;
in front of them they had a little cloud
and sang 'Hosanna' as they rose with it
(had there been other words, I would have told you).
Then I heard Love: 'I shall no longer hide
the truth from you. Come where our lady lies.'
My wild imaginings
led me to see my lady lying dead;
I looked at her, and then
ladies were drawing a veil over her face.
She had an air of joyful resignation;
it was as if she said: 'I am in peace.'

Then I became so humble in my sorrow,
seeing, in her, humility incarnate,
that I could say: 'O, Death, I hold you dear;
from now on you should put on graciousness
and change your scorn to sympathy for me,
since in my lady you have been at home.
See how I yearn to be one of your own:
I even look the way you would, alive.
Come, for my heart implores you!'
When the last rites were done, I left that place,
and when I was alone,
I raised my eyes toward Heaven, and declared:
'Blessed is he who sees you, lovely soul!'
You called to me just then, and I am grateful."

Donna pietosa e di novella etate,
   adorna assai di gentilezze umane,
   ch'era là 'v' io chiamava spesso Morte,
   veggendo li occhi miei pien di pietate,
   e ascoltando le parole vane,
   si mosse con paura a pianger forte.
   E altre donne, che si fuoro accorte
   di me per quella che meco piangia,
   fecer lei partir via,
   e appressarsi per farmi sentire.
   Qual dicea: "Non dormire,"
   e qual dicea: "Perché sì ti sconforte?"
   Allor lassai la nova fantasia,
   chiamando il nome de la donna mia.

Era la voce mia sì dolorosa
   e rotta sì da l'angoscia del pianto,
   ch'io solo intesi il nome nel mio core;
   e con tutta la vista vergognosa
   ch'era nel viso mio giunta cotanto,
   mi fece verso lor volgere Amore.
   Elli era tale a veder mio colore,
   che facea ragionar di morte altrui:
   "Deh, consoliam costui"
   pregava l'una l'altra umilemente;
   e dicevan sovente;
   "Che vedestù, che tu non hai valore?"
   E quando un poco confortato fui,
   io dissi: "Donne, dicerollo a vui.

Mentr'io pensava la mia frale vita,
   e vedea 'l suo durar com'è leggiero,
   piansemi Amor nel core, ove dimora;
   per che l'anima mia fu sì smarrita,
   che sospirando dicea nel pensero:
   'Ben converrà che la mia donna mora.'
   Io presi tanto smarrimento allora,
   ch'io chiusi li occhi vilmente gravati,
   e furon sì smagati
   li spiriti miei, che ciascun giva errando;

The New Life

e poscia imaginando,
di caunoscenza e di verità fora,
visi di donne m'apparver crucciati,
che mi dicean pur: 'Morra'ti, morra'ti.'

Poi vidi cose dubitose molte,
nel vano imaginare ov'io entrai;
ed esser mi parea non so in qual loco,
e veder donne andar per via disciolte,
qual lagrimando, e qual traendo guai,
che di tristizia saettavan foco.
Poi mi parve vedere a poco a poco
turbar lo sole e apparir la stella,
e pianger elli ed ella;
cader li augelli volando per l'are,
e la terra tremare;
ed omo apparve scolorito e fioco,
dicendomi: 'Che fai? non sai novella?
Morta è la donna tua, ch'era sì bella.'

Levava li occhi miei bagnati in pianti,
e vedea, che parean pioggia di manna,
li angeli che tornavan suso in cielo,
e una nuvoletta avean davanti,
dopo la qual gridavan tutti: Osanna;
e s'altro avesser detto, a voi dire'lo.
Allor diceva Amor: 'Più nol ti celo;
vieni a veder nostra donna che giace.'
Lo imaginar fallace
mi condusse a veder madonna morta;
e quand'io l'avea scorta,
vedea che donne la covrian d'un velo;
ed avea seco umilità verace,
che parea che dicesse: 'Io sono in pace.'

Io divenia nel dolor sì umile,
veggendo in lei tanta umiltà formata,
ch'io dicea: 'Morte, assai dolce ti tegno;
tu dei omai esser cosa gentile,
poi che tu se' ne la mia donna stata,
e dei aver pietate e non disdegno.

Vedi che sì desideroso vegno
d'esser de' tuoi, ch'io ti somiglio in fede.
Vieni, ché 'l cor te chiede.'
Poi mi partia, consumato ogne duolo;
e quand'io era solo,
dicea, guardando verso l'alto regno:
'Beato, anima bella, chi te vede!'
Voi mi chiamaste allor, vostra merzede."

This *canzone* has two sections. In the first, speaking to some unidentified person, I tell how I was aroused from a delirious dream by certain ladies, and how I promised to relate it to them; in the second I report what I told them. The second begins: *While I was brooding*. The first section divides into two parts: in the first I tell what certain ladies, and one particular lady, moved by my delirious state, said and did before I had returned to full consciousness; in the second I report what these ladies said to me after I had come out of my frenzy, and this part begins: *I called to her*. Then when I say: *While I was brooding*, I relate what I told them about my dream. And this section has two parts: in the first I describe the dream from beginning to end; in the second I tell at what point I was called by these ladies and, choosing my words discreetly, I thank them for waking me. And this part begins: *You called to me*.

XXIV

After this wild dream I happened one day to be sitting in a certain place deep in thought, when I felt a tremor begin in my heart, as if I were in the presence of my lady. Then a vision of Love came to me, and I seemed to see him coming from that place where my lady dwelt, and he seemed to say joyously from within my heart: "See that you bless the day that I took you captive; it is your duty to do so."

And it truly seemed to me that my heart was happy, so happy that it did not seem to be my heart because of this change. Shortly after my heart had said these words, speaking with the tongue of Love, I saw coming toward me a gentlewoman, noted for her beauty, who had been the much-loved lady of my best friend. Her name was Giovanna, but because of her beauty (as many believed) she had been given the name of Primavera, meaning Spring, and so she came to be called. And, looking behind her, I saw coming the miraculous Beatrice. These ladies passed close by me, one of them following the other, and it seemed that Love spoke in my heart and said: "The one in front is called Primavera only because of the way she comes today; for I inspired the giver of her name to call her Primavera, meaning 'she will come first' (*prima verrà*) on the day that Beatrice shows herself after the dream of her faithful one. And if you will also consider her real name, you will see that this too means 'she will come first', since the name Joan (*Giovanna*) comes from the name of that John (*Giovanni*) who preceded the True Light, saying: *Ego vox clamantis in deserto: parate viam Domini.*[11] After this, Love seemed to speak again and say these words: "Anyone of subtle discernment would call Beatrice Love, because she so greatly resembles me." Later, thinking this over, I decided to write a poem to my best friend (not mentioning certain things which I thought should not be revealed), whose heart, I believed, still admired the beauty of the radiant Primavera. And I wrote this sonnet which begins: *I felt a sleeping spirit.*

> I felt a sleeping spirit in my heart
>   awake to Love. And then from far away
>   I saw the Lord of love approaching me,
>   and hardly recognized him through his joy.

11. "I am the voice of one crying in the wilderness: prepare ye the way of the Lord."

Dante's Vita Nuova

"Think now of nothing but to honor me,"
I heard him say, and each word was a smile;
and as my master stayed awhile with me,
I looked along the way that he had come

and saw there Lady Joan and Lady Bice
    coming toward the place where I was standing:
    a miracle that led a miracle.
    And, as my memory recalls the scene,
Love said to me: "The first to come is Spring;
the one who is my image is called Love."

Io mi senti' svegliar dentro a lo core
    un spirito amoroso che dormia:
    e poi vidi venir da lungi Amore
    allegro sì, che appena il conoscia,
    dicendo: "Or pensa pur di farmi onore,"
    e 'n ciascuna parola sua ridia.
    E poco stando meco il mio segnore,
    guardando in quella parte onde venia,

io vidi monna Vanna e monna Bice
    venir inver lo loco là 'v'io era,
    l'una appresso de l'altra maraviglia;
    e sì come la mente mi ridice,
    Amor mi disse: "Quell'è Primavera,
    e quell'ha nome Amor, sì mi somiglia."

This sonnet has many parts. The first tells how I felt the
familiar tremor awaken in my heart, and how it seemed that
Love, joyful, coming from a far-away place, revealed himself
to me in my heart; the second records what Love seemed to
say to me in my heart, and how he looked; the third tells how,
after he had remained awhile with me, I saw and heard certain
things. The second part begins: *Think now*, the third: *and as
my master*. The third part divides into two: in the first I tell
what I saw, in the second I tell what I heard. The second part
begins: *Love said to me*.

XXV

At this point it may be that someone worthy of having every doubt cleared up could be puzzled at my speaking of Love as if it were a thing in itself, as if it were not only an intellectual substance, but also a bodily substance. This is patently false, for Love does not exist in itself as a substance, but is an accident in a substance. And that I speak of Love as if it possessed a body, further still, as if it were a human being, is shown by three things I say about it. I say that I saw it coming; and since "to come" implies locomotion, and since, according to the Philosopher, only a body may move from place to place by its own power, it is obvious that I assume Love to be a body. I also say that it laughed and even that it spoke—acts that would seem characteristic of a human being, especially that of laughing; and so it is clear that I assume love to be human. To clarify this matter suitably for my purpose, I shall begin by saying that, formerly, there were no love poets writing in the vernacular, the only love poets were those writing in Latin: among us (and this probably happened in other nations as it still happens in the case of Greece) it was not vernacular poets but learned poets who wrote about love. It is only recently that the first poets appeared who wrote in the vernacular; I call them "poets" for to compose rhymed verse in the vernacular is more or less the same as to compose poetry in Latin using classical meters.

And proof that it is but a short time since these poets first appeared is the fact that if we look into the Provençal and the Italian literatures, we shall not find any poems written more than a hundred and fifty years ago. The reason why a few ungifted poets acquired the fame of knowing how to compose is that they were the first who wrote poetry in the Italian language. The first poet to begin writing in the vernacular was moved to do so by a desire to make his words understandable to ladies who found Latin verses difficult to comprehend. And this is an argument against those who compose in the vernacular on a subject other than love, since composition in the vernacular was from the beginning intended for treating of love.

Since, in Latin, greater license is conceded to the poet than to the prose writer, and since these Italian writers are simply poets writing in the vernacular, we can conclude that it is fitting and reasonable that greater license be granted them than to other writers in the vernacular; therefore, if any image or coloring of words is conceded to the Latin poet, it should be conceded to the Italian poet. So, if we find that the Latin poets addressed inanimate objects in their writings, as if these objects had sense and reason, or made them address each other, and that they did this not only with real things but also with unreal things (that is: they have said, concerning things that do not exist, that they speak, and they have said that many an accident in substance speaks as if it were a substance and human), then it is fitting that the vernacular poet do the same—not, of course, without some reason, but with a motive that later can be explained in prose. That the Latin poets have written in the way I have just described can be seen in the case of Virgil, who says that Juno, a goddess hostile to the Trojans, spoke to Aeolus, god of the winds, in the first book of the *Aeneid: Eole, nanque tibi,*[12] and that this god answered her: *Tuus, o regina, quid optes explorare labor; michi iussa capessere fas est.*[13] This same poet has an inanimate thing speak to animate beings in the third book of the *Aeneid: Dardanide duri.*[14] In Lucan the animate being speaks to the inanimate object: *Multum, Roma, tamen debes civilibus armis.*[15] In Horace a man speaks to his own inspiration as if to another person, and not only are the

12. "Aeolus, for to you."
13. "Yours, O queen, is the task of determining your wishes; mine is the right to obey orders."
14. "You hardy Trojans."
15. "Much, Rome, do you owe, nevertheless, to the civil war."

words those of Horace but he gives them as if quoting from the good Homer, in this passage of his *Poetics: Dic michi, Musa, virum.*[16] In Ovid, Love speaks as if it were a human being, in the beginning of the book called *The Remedy of Love: Bella michi, video, bella parantur, ait.*[17]

From what has been said above, anyone who experiences difficulties in certain parts of this, my little book, can find a solution for them. So that some ungifted person may not be encouraged by my words to go too far, let me add that just as the Latin poets did not write in the way they did without a reason, so vernacular poets should not write in the same way without having some reason for writing as they do. For, if any one should dress his poem in images and rhetorical coloring and then, being asked to strip his poem of such dress in order to reveal its true meaning, would not be able to do so—this would be a veritable cause for shame. And my best friend and I are well acquainted with some who compose so clumsily.

XXVI

This most gracious lady of whom I have spoken in the preceding poems came into such widespread favor that, when she walked down the street, people ran to see her. This made me wonderfully happy. And when she passed by someone, such modesty filled his heart that he did not dare to raise his eyes or to return her greeting (many people, who have experienced this, could testify to it if anyone should not believe me). Crowned and clothed with humility, she would go her way, taking no glory from what she heard and saw. Many would say after she had passed: "This is no woman, this is one of the most beautiful angels of Heaven." And others

16. "Tell me, Muse, of the man."
17. "Wars against me I see, wars are preparing, he says."

would say: "She is a miracle! Blessed be the Lord who can work so wondrously." Let me say that she showed such decorum and was possessed of such charming qualities that those who looked at her experienced a pure and sweet delight, such that they were unable to describe it; and there was no one who could look at her without immediately sighing. These and still more marvelous things were the result of her powers. Thinking about this, and wishing to take up again the theme of her praise, I decided to write something which would describe her magnificent and beneficent efficacy, so that not only those who could see her with their own eyes, but others, as well, might know of her whatever can be said in words. And so I wrote this sonnet which begins: *Such sweet decorum.*

> Such sweet decorum and such gentle grace
>   attend my lady's greeting as she moves
>   that lips can only tremble into silence,
>   and eyes dare not attempt to gaze at her.
>   Moving, benignly clothed in humility,
>   untouched by all the praise along her way,
>   she seems to be a creature come from Heaven
>   to earth, to manifest a miracle.
>
> Miraculously gracious to behold,
>   her sweetness reaches, through the eyes, the heart
>   (who has not felt this cannot understand),
>   and from her lips it seems there moves a gracious
>   spirit, so deeply loving that it glides
>   into the souls of men, whispering: "Sigh!"

> *Tanto gentile e tanto onesta pare*
>   *la donna mia quand'ella altrui saluta,*
>   *ch'ogne lingua deven tremando muta,*
>   *e li occhi no l'ardiscon di guardare.*
>   *Ella si va, sentendosi laudare,*
>   *benignamente d'umiltà vestuta,*
>   *e par che sia una cosa venuta*
>   *da cielo in terra a miracol mostrare.*

The New Life

Mostrasi sì piacente a chi la mira,
  che dà per li occhi una dolcezza al core,
  che 'ntender no la può chi no la prova;
  e par che de la sua labbia si mova
  un spirito soave pien d'amore,
  che va dicendo a l'anima: "Sospira!"

This sonnet is so easy to understand from what has preceded that it has no need of divisions. And so, leaving it aside, let me say that my lady came into such high favor that not only she was honored and praised, but also many other ladies were honored and praised because of her. Having observed this and wishing to make it evident to those who had not seen it, I decided to compose something else in which this would be brought out. I then wrote this next sonnet, which begins: *He sees an affluence,* telling how her virtuous power affected other ladies, as appears in the divisions.

He sees an affluence of joy ideal
  who sees my lady, in the midst of other ladies;
  those ladies who accompany her are moved
  to thank God for this sweet gift of His grace.
  Her beauty has the power of such magic,
  it never rouses other ladies' envy,
  instead, it makes them want to be like her:
  clothed in love and faith and graciousness.

The sight of her creates humility;
  and not only is she splendid in her beauty,
  but every lady near her shares her praise.
  Her every act is graciousness in essence;
  there is no one can recall her to his mind
  and not sigh in an ecstasy of love.

Vede perfettamente onne salute
  chi la mia donna tra le donne vede;
  quelle che vanno con lei son tenute
  di bella grazia a Dio render merzede.
  E sua bieltate è di tanta vertute,

che nulla invidia a l'altre ne procede,
anzi le face andar seco vestute
di gentilezza, d'amore e di fede.

La vista sua fa onne cosa umile;
e non fa sola sé parer piacente,
ma ciascuna per lei receve onore.
Ed è ne li atti suoi tanto gentile,
che nessun la si può recare a mente,
che non sospiri in dolcezza d'amore.

This sonnet has three parts. In the first I tell in whose company this lady seemed most admirable; in the second I tell how
desirable it was to be in her company; in the third I speak of
those things which she miraculously brought about in others.
The second part begins: *those ladies who;* the third: *Her
beauty.* This last part divides into three. In the first part I tell
what she brought about in ladies, that was known only to them;
in the second I tell what she did for them as seen by others;
in the third I say that she miraculously affected not only ladies
but all persons, and not only while they were in her presence
but also when they recalled her to mind. The second begins:
The sight of her; the third: *Her every act.*

XXVII

After this I began one day thinking over
what I had said about my lady in these last two sonnets and,
realizing that I had not said anything about the effect she had
on me at the present time, it seemed to me that I had spoken
insufficiently. And so I decided to write a poem telling how I
seemed to be disposed to her influence, and how her miraculous
power worked in me; and believing I would not be able to
describe this within the limits of a sonnet, I immediately started
to write a *canzone* which begins: *So long a time.*

So long a time has Love kept me a slave
  and in his lordship fully seasoned me,
  that even though at first I felt him harsh,
  now tender is his power in my heart.
  But when he takes my strength away from me
  so that my spirits seem to wander off,
  my fainting soul is overcome with sweetness,
  and the color of my face begins to fade.

Then Love starts working in me with such power
  he turns my spirits into ranting beggars,
  and, rushing out, they call
  upon my lady, pleading in vain for kindness.
  This happens every time she looks at me,
  yet she herself is kind beyond belief.

> *Sì lungiamente m'ha tenuto Amore*
> *e costumato a la sua segnoria,*
> *che sì com'elli m'era forte in pria,*
> *così mi sta soave ora nel core.*
> *Però quando mi tolle sì 'l valore,*
> *che li spiriti par che fuggan via,*
> *allor sente la frale anima mia*
> *tanta dolcezza, che 'l viso ne smore.*

> *Poi prende Amore in me tanta vertute,*
> *che fa li miei spiriti gir parlando,*
> *ed escon for chiamando*
> *la donna mia, per darmi più salute.*
> *Questo m'avvene ovunque ella mi vede,*
> *e sì è cosa umil, che nol si crede.*

XXVIII

Quomodo sedet sola civitas plena populo!
facta est quasi vidua domina gentium![18] I was still engaged

18. "How doth the city sit solitary that was full of people! How is
she become a widow, she that was great among the nations!"

in composing this *canzone*, in fact I had completed only the stanza written above, when the God of Justice called this most gracious one to glory under the banner of that blessèd Queen, the Virgin Mary, whose name was always uttered with the greatest reverence by the blessèd Beatrice. And even though the reader might expect me to say something now about her departure from us, it is not my intention to do so here for three reasons. The first is that such a discussion does not fit into the plan of this little book, if we consider the preface which precedes it; the second is that, even if this had been my intention, the language at my command would not yet suffice to deal with the theme as it deserves; the third is that even supposing that the first two reasons did not exist, it still would not be proper for me to treat the theme since this would entail praising myself —which is the most reprehensible thing one can do. Therefore, I leave this subject to some other commentator.

But since the number nine has appeared many times in what I have already written (which clearly could not happen without a reason), and since in her departure this number seemed to play an important part, it is fitting that I say something here concerning this, inasmuch as it seems to fit in with my plan. And so I shall first speak of the part it played in her departure, and then I shall give some reasons why this number was so close to her.

XXIX

Let me begin by saying that if one counts in the Arabian way, her most noble soul departed this life during the first hour of the ninth day of the month, and if one counts the way they do in Syria, she departed in the ninth month of the year, the first month there being Tixryn the First, which for us is October. And, according to our own way of reckoning, she departed in that year of our Christian era (that is in the year of Our Lord) in which the perfect number had been completed nine times in that century in which she had been placed in this world: she was a Christian of the Thirteenth Century. One reason why this number was in such harmony with her might be this: since, according to Ptolemy and according to Christian truth, there are nine heavens that move, and since, according to widespread astrological opinion, these heavens affect the earth below according to the relations they have to one another, this number was in harmony with her to make it understood that at her birth all nine of the moving heavens were in perfect relationship to one another. But this is just one reason. If anyone thinks more subtly and according to infallible truth, it will be clear that this number was she herself—that is, by analogy. What I mean to say is this: the number three is the root of nine for, without any other number, multiplied by itself, it gives nine: it is quite clear that three times three is nine. Therefore, if three is the sole factor of nine, and the sole factor of miracles is three, that is, Father, Son, and Holy Spirit, who are Three in One, then this lady was accompanied by the number nine so that it might be understood that she was a nine, or a miracle, whose root, namely that of the miracle, is the miraculous Trinity itself. Perhaps someone more subtle than I could find a still more subtle explanation, but this is the one which I see and which pleases me the most.

XXX

After she had departed from this world, the aforementioned city was left as if a widow, stripped of all dignity, and I, still weeping in this barren city, wrote to the princes of the land describing its condition, taking my opening words from the prophet Jeremiah where he says: *Quomodo sedet sola civitas.*[19] And I mention this quotation now so that everyone will understand why I cited these words earlier: it was to serve as a heading for the new material that follows. And if someone should wish to reproach me for not including the rest of the letter, my excuse is this: since it was my intention from the beginning to write in the vernacular, and since the words which follow those just quoted are all in Latin, it would be contrary to my intention if I were to include them. And I know that my best friend, for whom I write this book, shares my opinion: that it be written entirely in the vernacular.

XXXI

After my eyes had wept for some time and were so wept out that they could no longer relieve my sadness, I thought of trying to relieve it with some sorrowful words; and I decided to compose a *canzone* in which, lamenting, I would speak of her who was the cause of the grief that was destroying my soul. Then I started writing a *canzone* which begins: *The eyes grieving*. And in order that this *canzone* may seem to remain all the more widowed after it has come to an end, I shall divide it before I copy it. And from now on I shall follow this method.

Let me say that this sad little song has three parts. The first is an introduction; in the second I speak of her; in the third I sadly address the *canzone* itself. The second part begins: *Beatrice has gone*, the third: *Now go your way*. The first part divides further into three: in the first I say why I am moved to speak; in the second I tell who it is I wish to speak to; in the third I tell who it is I wish to speak about. The second begins: *Since I remember*; the third: *My words will be.* Then

19. "How doth the city sit solitary."

when I say: *Beatrice has gone,* I am speaking about her, and of this I make two parts: first I tell the reason why she was taken from us; then I tell how someone laments her departure, and I begin this part with the words: *And once withdrawn.* This part further divides into three: in the first I tell who it is that does not mourn her; in the second I tell who it is that does mourn her; in the third I speak of my own condition. The second begins: *But grief,* the third: *Weeping and pain.* Then when I say: *Now go your way,* I am speaking to this *canzone,* designating the ladies to whom it is to go and with whom it is to stay.

> The eyes grieving out of pity for the heart,
>   while weeping, have endured great suffering,
>   so that they are defeated, tearless eyes.
>   And now, if I should want to vent that grief,
>   which gradually leads me to my death,
>   I must express myself in anguished words.
>   Since I remember how I loved to speak
>   about my lady when she was alive,
>   addressing, gracious ladies, you alone,
>   I will not speak to others,
>   but only to a lady's tender heart.
>   My words will be a dirge, for they tell how
>   she suddenly ascended into Heaven,
>   and how she left Love here to grieve with me.
>
> Beatrice has gone home to highest Heaven,
>   into the peaceful realm where angels live;
>   she is with them; she has left you, ladies, here.
>   No quality of heat or cold took her
>   away from us, as is the fate of others;
>   it was her great unselfishness alone.
>   For the pure light of her humility
>   shone through the heavens with such radiance,
>   it even made the Lord Eternal marvel;
>   and then a sweet desire
>   moved Him to summon up such blessedness;

and from down here He had her come to Him,
because He knew this wretched life on earth
did not deserve to have her gracious presence.

And once withdrawn from her enchanting form,
the tender soul, perfectly full of grace,
now lives with glory in her rightful place.
Who speaks of her and does not speak in tears
has a vile heart, insensitive as stone
which never can be visited by love.
No evil heart could have sufficient wit
to conceive in any way what she was like,
and so it has no urge to weep from grief.
But grief comes and the wish
to sigh and then to die a death of tears
(and consolation is denied forever)
to anyone who pictures in his thoughts
that which she was and how she went from us.

I breathe deep sighs of anguished desolation
when memory brings to my weary mind
the image of that one who split my heart;
and many times, while contemplating death,
so sweet a longing for it comes to me,
it drains away the color from my face.
When this imagining has hold of me,
bitter affliction binds me on all sides,
and I begin to tremble from the pain.
I am not what I am,
and so my shame drives me away from others;
and then I weep alone in my lamenting,
calling to Beatrice: "Can you be dead?"
And just to call her name restores my soul.

Weeping and pain and many anguished sighs
torment my heart each time I am alone,
and if some one should hear me, he would suffer;
just what my life has been since the hour when
my lady passed into the timeless realm,
there is not any tongue could tell of it.
And so, my ladies, even if I tried,

The New Life

I could not tell you what I have become;
my bitter life is constant suffering,
a life so much abased
that every man who sees my deathly face
seems to be telling me: "I cast you out!"
But what I have become my lady knows;
I still have hope that she will show me grace.

Now go your way in tears, sad little song,
and find once more the ladies and the maidens
to whom your sister poems
were sent as messengers of happiness;
and you who are the daughter of despair,
go look for them, wearing my misery.

Li occhi dolenti per pietà del core
hanno di lagrimar sofferta pena,
sì che per vinti son remasi omai.
Ora, s'i' voglio sfogar lo dolore,
che a poco a poco a la morte mi mena,
convenemi parlar traendo guai.
E perché me ricorda ch'io parlai
de la mia donna, mentre che vivia,
donne gentili, volentier con vui,
non voi parlare altrui,
se non a cor gentil che in donna sia;
e dicerò di lei piangendo, pui
che si n'è gita in ciel subitamente,
e ha lasciato Amor meco dolente.

Ita n'è Beatrice in l'alto cielo,
nel reame ove li angeli hanno pace,
e sta con loro, e voi, donne, ha lassate:
no la ci tolse qualità di gelo
né di calore, come l'altre face,
ma solo fue sua gran benignitate;
ché luce de la sua umilitate
passò li cieli con tanta vertute,
che fè maravigliar l'etterno sire,
sì che dolce disire
lo giunse di chiamar tanta salute;

Dante's Vita Nuova

e fella di qua giù a sé venire,
perchè vedea ch'esta vita noiosa
non era degna di sì gentil cosa.

Partissi de la sua bella persona
piena di grazia l'anima gentile,
ed èssi gloriosa in loco degno.
Chi no la piange, quando ne ragiona,
core ha di pietra sì malvagio e vile,
ch'entrar no i puote spirito benegno.
Non è di cor villan sì alto ingegno,
che possa imaginar di lei alquanto,
e però no li ven di pianger doglia:
ma ven tristizia e voglia
di sospirare e di morir di pianto,
e d'onne consolar l'anima spoglia
chi vede nel pensero alcuna volta
quale ella fue, e com'ella n'è tolta.

Dannomi angoscia li sospiri forte,
quando 'l pensero ne la mente grave
mi reca quella che m'ha 'l cor diviso:
e spesse fiate pensando a la morte,
venemene un disio tanto soave,
che mi tramuta lo color nel viso.
E quando 'l maginar mi ven ben fiso,
giugnemi tanta pena d'ogne parte,
ch'io mi riscuoto per dolor ch'i' sento;
e sì fatto divento,
che da le genti vergogna mi parte.
Poscia piangendo, sol nel mio lamento
chiamo Beatrice, e dico: "Or se' tu morta?"
e mentre ch'io la chiamo, me conforta.

Pianger di doglia e sospirar d'angoscia
mi strugge 'l core ovunque sol mi trovo,
sì che ne 'ncrescerebbe a chi m'audesse:
e quale è stata la mia vita, poscia
che la mia donna andò nel secol novo,
lingua non è che dicer lo sapesse:
e però, donne mie, pur ch'io volesse,

The New Life

non vi saprei io dir ben quel ch'io sono,
sì mi fa travagliar l'acerba vita;
la quale è sì 'nvilita,
che ogn'om par che mi dica: "Io t'abbandono,"
veggendo la mia labbia tramortita.
Ma qual ch'io sia la mia donna il si vede,
e io ne spero ancor da lei merzede.

Pietosa mia canzone, or va piangendo;
e ritruova le donne e le donzelle
a cui le tue sorelle
erano usate di portar letizia;
e tu, che se' figliuola di tristizia,
vatten disconsolata a star con elle.

XXXII

After this *canzone* was composed, a
person came to see me who, according to degrees of friendship,
was second after my best friend. And he was so closely related
to this glorious lady that no one else was more so. After we
had talked together for a while, he begged me to write something for him about a lady who had died, disguising his motives
so as to appear to be speaking of a different one who had recently died. I, being quite aware that he was speaking only
about that blessèd one, told him I would do as he asked. Then,
thinking it over, I decided to compose a sonnet, to be sent to
this friend of mine, in which I would express my sorrow in
such a way that it would seem to be his.

And so I wrote this sonnet which begins: *Now come to me.*
It consists of two parts: in the first I call upon Love's faithful
to listen to me, in the second I speak of my wretched condition. The second part begins: *the sighs that issue.*

Now come to me and listen to my sighs,
    O gracious hearts (it is the wish of Pity),

the sighs that issue in despondency.
But for their help I would have died of grief,
because my eyes would be in debt to me,
owing much more than they could hope to pay
by weeping so profusely for my lady
that, mourning her, my heart might be relieved.

And sighs of mine shall ceaselessly be heard
calling upon my lady (who is gone
to dwell where worth like hers is merited),
or breathing their contempt for this our life,
as if they were the mournful soul itself
abandoned by its hope of happiness.

Venite a intender li sospiri miei,
oi cor gentili, ché pietà 'l disia:
li quai disconsolati vanno via,
e s'e' non fosser, di dolor morrei,
però che li occhi mi sarebber rei,
molte fiate più ch'io non vorria,
lasso, di pianger sì la donna mia,
che sfogasser lo cor, piangendo lei.

Voi udirete lor chiamar sovente
la mia donna gentil, che si n'è gita
al secol degno de la sua vertute;
e dispregiar talora questa vita
in persona de l'anima dolente
abbandonata de la sua salute.

XXXIII

After I had composed this sonnet, I
realized, thinking more about the person to whom I intended
to give it as an expression of his own feelings, that the poem
might seem a poor and empty favor for anyone so closely
related to my lady now in glory. So, before giving him the
sonnet included above, I wrote two stanzas of a *canzone*, one
of them truly in behalf of my friend and the other for myself,

although to an unobservant reader they would both appear to speak for the same person. Anyone who examines them closely, however, sees clearly that different persons are speaking, since one does not call her his lady while the other does, as the reader may see for himself. I gave him this *canzone* and the sonnet included above, telling him that it was all written for him alone.

This *canzone* begins: *Each time*, and it has two parts. In one of them, in the first stanza, it is this good friend of mine and close relative of hers who laments; in the second I myself lament, that is, in the other stanza which begins: *Then there is blended*. And so it is clear that two people are lamenting in this *canzone*, one of whom grieves as a brother, the other as Love's servant.

> Each time the painful thought comes to my mind
>   that I shall nevermore
>   behold the lady I will always mourn,
> my grieving memory summons up such grief
> swelling within my heart,
> that I must say: "Why linger here, my soul?
> The torments you will be subjected to
> in this life which already you detest,
> weigh heavily upon my fearful mind."
> Then calling upon Death,
> as I would call on lovely, soothing Peace,
> I say with yearning love: "Please come to me."
> And I am jealous of whoever dies.
>
> Then there is blended out of all my sighs
>   a chorus of beseeching,
>   begging continuously for Death to come.
> All my desires have centered on this wish
> since that day when my lady
> was taken from me by Death's cruelty.
> This is because the beauty of her grace,
> withdrawing from the sight of men forever,
> became transformed to beauty of the soul,

diffusing through the heavens
a light of love that greets the angels there,
moving their subtle, lofty intellects
to marvel at this miracle of grace.

Quantunque volte, lasso, mi rimembra
ch'io non debbo già mai
veder la donna ond'io vo sì dolente,
tanto dolore intorno 'l cor m'assembra
la dolorosa mente,
ch'io dico: "Anima mia, ché non ten vai?
chè li tormenti che tu porterai
nel secol, che t'è già tanto noioso,
mi fan pensoso di paura forte."
Ond'io chiamo la Morte,
come soave e dolce mio riposo;
e dico "Vieni a me" con tanto amore,
che sono astioso di chiunque more.

E' si raccoglie ne li miei sospiri
un sono di pietate,
che va chiamando Morte tuttavia:
a lei si volser tutti i miei disiri,
quando la donna mia
fu giunta da la sua crudelitate;
perché 'l piacere de la sua bieltate,
partendo sé da la nostra veduta,
divenne spiritual bellezza grande,
che per lo cielo spande
luce d'amor, che li angeli saluta,
e lo intelletto loro alto, sottile
face maravigliar, sì v'è gentile.

XXXIV

On the day which completed a year
since that lady had become a citizen of the Eternal Life, I was
sitting in a place where, thinking of her, I was drawing an
angel on some panels. And while I was drawing, I looked up

and saw around me some men to whom all consideration was due. They were watching what I was doing and, as I was then told, they had already been there some time before I became aware of their presence. When I saw them, I stood up and, greeting them, I said: "Someone was with me just now; that is why I was so deep in thought." After they left, I returned to my work of drawing figures of angels and, while I was doing this, the idea came to me to write some poetry, in the nature of an anniversary poem, and to address it to those men who had just been with me. And so I wrote this sonnet which begins: *Into my mind*, and which has two beginnings; for this reason I divide it first according to the one, and then according to the other.

Now, according to the first beginning, this sonnet has three parts. In the first I say that this lady was already in my memory; in the second I tell what Love, therefore, did to me; in the third I speak of the effects of Love. The second begins: *Love, who perceived*, the third: *Lamenting*. This last part divides into two: in the first I say that all my sighs came forth speaking; in the second I state that some spoke different words from the others. The second begins: *but those*. According to the other beginning this sonnet divides in the same way, except that in the first part I tell when it was that this lady came into my memory, while in the first beginning I do not.

First beginning
Into my mind had come the gracious image
    of the lady for whom Love still sheds tears,
    was called by His most lofty Majesty
    to the calm realm of Heaven where Mary reigns.

Primo cominciamento
Era venuta ne la mente mia
    la gentil donna che per suo valore
    fu posta da l'altissimo signore
    nel ciel de l'umiltate, ov'è Maria.

Dante's Vita Nuova

Second beginning

Into my mind had come the gracious image
 of the lady for whom Love still sheds tears,
 just when you were attracted by her virtue
 to come and see what I was doing there.
 Love, who perceived her presence in my mind,
 and was aroused within my ravaged heart,
 commanded all my sighs: "Go forth from here!"
 And each one started on his grieving way.

Lamenting, they came pouring from my heart,
 together in a single voice (that often
 brings painful tears to my melancholy eyes);
 but those escaping with the greatest pain
 were saying: "This day, O intellect sublime,
 completes a year since you rose heavenward."

Secondo cominciamento
Era venuta ne la mente mia
 quella donna gentil cui piange Amore
 entro 'n quel punto che lo suo valore
 vi trasse a riguardar quel ch'eo facia.
 Amor, che ne la mente la sentia,
 s'era svegliato nel destrutto core,
 e dicea a' sospiri: "Andate fore,"
 per che ciascun dolente si partia.

Piangendo uscivan for de lo mio petto
 con una voce che sovente mena
 la lagrime dogliose a li occhi tristi.
 Ma quei che n'uscian for con maggior pena,
 venian dicendo: "Oi nobile intelletto,
 oggi fa l'anno che nel ciel salisti."

XXXV

Sometime afterward, when I happened
to be in a place which recalled past times, I was in a very
pensive mood, and I was moved by such painful thoughts that

I must have had a frightening expression of distress on my face. Becoming aware of my terrible condition, I looked around to see if anyone were watching me. And I saw at a window a gracious lady, young and exceedingly beautiful, who was looking down at me so compassionately, to judge from her appearance, that all pity seemed to be concentrated in her. And because whenever an unhappy person sees someone take pity on him, he is all the more easily moved to tears, as if taking pity on himself, so I immediately felt the tears start to come. Fearing that I was revealing all the wretchedness in my life, I turned away from her eyes and left that place. And later I said to myself: "It must surely be true that with that compassionate lady there is present most noble Love."

And so I decided to write a sonnet which I would address to her and in which I would include everything that has been narrated in this account. And since, because of this account, its meaning is sufficiently clear, I shall not divide it. The sonnet begins: *With my own eyes.*

> With my own eyes I saw how much compassion
> there was in the expression of your face,
> when you saw how I looked and how I acted
> (it is my grief that forces me to this).
> Then I became aware that you had seen
> into the nature of my darkened life,
> and this aroused a fear within my heart
> of showing in my eyes my wretched state.
>
> I fled, then, from your presence as I felt
> the tears begin to overflow my heart
> that was exalted at the sight of you.
> Later, within my anguished soul, I said:
> "There must dwell with that lady that same Love
> that makes me go about like this in tears."

> *Videro li occhi miei quanta pietate*
> *era apparita in la vostra figura*
> *quando guardaste li atti e la statura*

ch'io faccio per dolor molte fiate.
Allor m'accorsi che voi pensavate
la qualità de la mia vita oscura,
sì che mi giunse ne lo cor paura
di dimostrar con li occhi mia viltate.

E tolsimi dinanzi a voi, sentendo
che si movean le lagrime dal core,
ch'era sommosso da la vostra vista.
Io dicea poscia ne l'anima trista:
"Ben è con quella donna quello Amore
lo qual mi face andar così piangendo."

XXXVI

After that, it always happened that whenever this lady saw me, her face would become compassionate and turn a pale color almost like that of love, so that many times I was reminded of my most noble lady who always had a similar coloring. And many times when I was unable to vent my sadness by weeping, I used to go to see this compassionate lady whose expression alone was able to bring tears to my eyes. And so the urge came to me to write some other poetry addressed to her, and I composed this sonnet which begins: *Color of love.* And because of what has just been said, it is clear without analysis.

Color of love, expression of compassion,
    have never so miraculously come
    to the face of any lady when she gazed
    at eyes susceptible of anguished tears,
    as they came to your face whenever I
    stood in your presence with my grieving face;
    and something comes to mind because of you:
    a thought that makes me fear my heart will split.

I cannot keep my devastated eyes
    from looking ever and again at you

because of the desire they have to weep;
and you intensify their longing so
that they consume themselves in helpless yearning,
for, in your presence, they cannot weep tears.

Color d'amore e di pietà sembianti
non preser mai così mirabilmente
viso di donna, per veder sovente
occhi gentili o dolorosi pianti,
come lo vostro qualora davanti
vedetevi la mia labbia dolente;
sì che per voi mi ven cosa a la mente,
ch'io temo forte non lo cor si schianti.

Eo non posso tener li occhi distrutti
che non reguardin voi spesse fiate,
per desiderio di pianger ch'elli hanno:
e voi crescete sì lor volontate,
che de la voglia si consuman tutti,
ma lagrimar dinanzi a voi non sanno.

XXXVII

The sight of this lady had now brought
me to the point that my eyes began to enjoy the sight of her
too much; I often became angry at myself because of it, and
I felt I was very contemptible. So, many times I would curse
the wantonness of my eyes, and in my thoughts I would say
to them: "You used to make anyone weep who saw your sad
state, and now it seems you want to forget about all that because of this lady who gazes at you, who gazes at you only
because of her grief for the glorious lady whom you used to
mourn. Do whatever you will, but I shall remind you of her
many times, damned eyes, for never, before death comes, should
your tears have ceased." And after I had said this to myself,
addressing my eyes, I was overcome by sighs, deep and

anguished. I felt that this conflict which I was having with myself should not remain known solely to the wretch that experienced it, so I decided to compose a sonnet describing this terrible condition.

I wrote the sonnet which begins: *The bitter tears*. It has two parts: in the first I tell my eyes what my heart was saying to me; in the second I prevent any confusion by explaining who is speaking this way, and this part begins: *This is what my heart*. The sonnet could very well be analyzed further, but this would be superfluous, as the preceding account makes its meaning quite clear.

"The bitter tears that you once used to shed,
   you, my eyes, and for so long a time,
   have made the tears of other persons flow
   for pity's sake, as you yourselves have seen.
And now it seems to me you would forget,
   if I were so disloyal for my part
   as to give you any chance, by not forever
   reminding you of her whom once you mourned.

I think about your infidelity,
   and I am frightened; I have come to dread
   the lady's face that often looks at you.
   Until death kills your sight, never should you
   forget your gracious lady who is dead."
This is what my heart says—and then it sighs.

"*L'amaro lagrimar che voi faceste,*
   oi occhi miei, così lunga stagione,
   facea lagrimar l'altre persone
   de la pietate, come voi vedeste.
Ora mi par che voi l'obliereste,
   s'io fosse dal mio lato sì fellone,
   ch'i' non ven disturbasse ogne cagione,
   membrandovi colei cui voi piangeste.

La vostra vanità mi fa pensare,
   e spaventami sì, ch'io temo forte

del viso d'una donna che vi mira.
Voi non dovreste mai, se non per morte,
la vostra donna, ch'è morta, obliare."
Così dice 'l meo core, e poi sospira.

XXXVIII

When, once again, I returned to see this
lady, the sight of her had such a strange effect on me that often
I thought of her as someone I liked too much. I thought of her
in this way: "This is a gracious, beautiful, young, and discreet
lady, and perhaps through the will of Love she has appeared
in order that my life may find peace." Often I thought in still
more loving terms, so much so that the heart consented to it,
that is to the loving feeling. And when I had consented to this,
I reconsidered, as if moved by reason, and I said to myself:
"God, what kind of thought is this that tries to console me so
basely and scarcely allows me to think about anything else?"
Then another thought arose and said to me: "Since you have
endured so many tribulations, why do you not try to escape
further bitter suffering? You see that this is an inspiration of
Love, which brings amorous desires into our presence, and it
proceeds from so gracious a source as the eyes of the lady who
has shown us so much compassion." Finally, having battled
like this within myself many times, I wished to write more
poetry about it, and since in the battle of the thoughts those
won which spoke in the lady's favor, it seemed right that I
address myself to her. And I wrote this sonnet which begins:
A thought, gracious; and I say "gracious" in so far as it involved a gracious lady, for in all other respects it was most
base.

In this sonnet I divide myself into two parts according to
the way my thoughts were divided. One part I call *heart,* that
is desire; the other, *soul,* that is reason; and I tell what one says

to the other. That it is justifiable to call desire *heart* and reason *soul* is certainly clear to those persons that I wish my procedure to be clear to. It is true that in the preceding sonnet I take the part of the heart against the eyes, and this seems contrary to what I say in this sonnet. So let me state that in the preceding sonnet, too, the heart stands for desire, since my greatest desire was still that of remembering my most gracious lady rather than of gazing at this one—even though I did have some desire for her then; but it seemed slight. And so it is evident that the one interpretation is not contrary to the other.

This sonnet has three parts. In the first I tell this lady how my desire turns completely toward her; in the second I tell how the soul, that is reason, speaks to the heart, that is desire; in the third I tell how the heart replies. The second part begins: *The soul says*, the third: *The heart replies*.

> A thought, gracious because it speaks of you,
>   comes frequently to dwell awhile with me,
>   and so melodiously speaks of love,
>   it talks the heart into surrendering.
>   The soul says to the heart: "Who is this one
>   that comes with consolation for our mind,
>   possessing such outrageous strength that he
>   will not let other thoughts remain with us?"
>
> The heart replies: "O reasonable soul,
>   this is a spirit of Love, tender and new,
>   who brings all his desires here to me;
>   all his intensity, his very life,
>   have come from that compassionate one's eyes
>   who was distressed about our martyrdom."

> *Gentil pensero che parla di vui*
>   *sen vene a dimorar meco sovente,*
>   *e ragiona d'amor sì dolcemente,*
>   *che face consentir lo core in lui.*
>   *L'anima dice al cor: "Chi è costui,*
>   *che vene a consolar la nostra mente,*

> ed è la sua vertù tanto possente,
> ch'altro penser non lascia star con nui?"

> *Ei le risponde: "Oi anima pensosa,*
> *questi è uno spiritel novo d'amore,*
> *che reca innanzi me li suoi desiri;*
> *e la sua vita, e tutto 'l suo valore,*
> *mosse de li occhi di quella pietosa*
> *che si turbava de' nostri martiri."*

XXXIX

One day, about the ninth hour, there arose in me against this adversary of reason a powerful vision, in which I seemed to see that glorious Beatrice clothed in those crimson garments with which she first appeared to my eyes, and she seemed young, of the same age as when I first saw her. Then I began to think about her and, remembering her in the sequence of past times, my heart began to repent painfully of the desire by which it so basely let itself be possessed for some time, contrary to the constancy of reason; and once I had discarded this evil desire, all my thoughts turned back to their most gracious Beatrice.

Let me say that, from then on, I began to think of her so deeply with my whole shameful heart that my many sighs were proof of it, for all of them on issuing forth would repeat what my heart was saying, that is, the name of that most gracious one and how she departed from us. And many times it happened that some thoughts were so filled with anguish that I would forget what I was thinking and where I was. By this rekindling of sighs, the tears which had subsided began to flow again, so that my eyes seemed to be two objects whose only desire was to weep. And often it occurred that after continuous weeping a purplish color encircled my eyes, as often appears in one who has endured affliction. In this way they were justly rewarded for their inconstancy, and from then on they could not look at any person who might look back at them in such a way as to encourage again a similar inclination. And in order for it to be known that such an evil desire and foolish temptation had been destroyed, so that the poetry I had written before would raise no question, I decided to write a sonnet which should contain the essence of what I have just related. And I wrote: *Alas! By the full force,* and I said "Alas!" because I was ashamed of the fact that my eyes had been so faithless.

I do not divide this sonnet because its reason for existence makes it clear enough.

Alas! By the full force of countless sighs
    born of the thoughts that overflow my heart,
    the eyes are vanquished, and they do not dare
    to return the glance of anyone who sees them.
    They have become twin symbols of my yearning,
    to show, by shedding tears, how much I suffer;
    and many times they mourn so much that Love
    encircles them with martyrdom's red crown.

These meditations and the sighs I breathe
    become so anguishing within the heart
    that Love, who dwells there, faints, he is so tortured;
    for on those thoughts and sighs of lamentation
    the sweet name of my lady is inscribed,
    with many words relating to her death.

Lasso! per forza di molti sospiri,
    che nascon de' penser che son nel core,
    li occhi son vinti, e non hanno valore
    di riguardar persona che li miri.
    E fatti son che paion due disiri
    di lagrimare e di mostrar dolore,
    e spesse volte piangon sì, ch'Amore
    li 'ncerchia di corona di martiri.

Questi pensieri, e li sospir ch'eo gitto,
diventan ne lo cor sì angosciosi,
ch'Amor vi tramortisce, sì lien dole;
però ch'elli hanno in lor li dolorosi
quel dolce nome di madonna scritto,
e de la morte sua molte parole.

XL

After this period of distress, during the season when many people go to see the blessed image that Jesus Christ left us as a visible sign of his most beautiful countenance (which my lady beholds in glory), it happened that some pilgrims were going down a street which runs through the center of the city where the most gracious lady was born, lived and died. These pilgrims, it seemed to me, were very pensive as they moved along and I, thinking about them, said to myself: "These pilgrims seem to come from distant parts, and I do not believe that they have ever heard this lady mentioned; they know nothing about her—in fact, their thoughts are centered on other things than what surrounds them; perhaps they are thinking of their friends far away whom we cannot know." Then I said to myself: "I know that, if they were from a neighboring town, they would in some way appear distressed as they passed through the center of the desolated city." Again I said to myself: "If I could detain them for awhile, I know I could make them weep before they left this city, for I would speak words that would make anyone weep who heard them." After they had passed from my sight, I decided to compose a sonnet in which I would reveal what I had said to myself.

And, to make the effect more pathetic, I decided to write it as if I were speaking to them, and I composed this sonnet which begins: *Ah, pilgrims.* And I used the word "pilgrims" in its general sense, for the term can be understood in two ways, one general and the other specific. In the general sense a pilgrim is one who is traveling outside of his own country; in a specific sense "pilgrim" means only one who travels to or returns from the house of St. James. And it is to be known further that there are three ways that those who travel in the service of the Most High may be accurately designated. They are called "palmers" who cross the sea to the Holy Land and often bring back palms; they are called "pilgrims" who travel to the house of Galicia, because the tomb of St. James is farther away from his own country than that of any other apostle; they are called "Romers" who travel to Rome, where those whom I call "pilgrims" were going.

I will not divide this sonnet since its reason for existence makes it clear enough.

> Ah, pilgrims, moving pensively along,
>   thinking, perhaps, of things at home you miss,
>   could the land you come from be so far away
>   (as anyone might guess from your appearance)
>   that you show no signs of grief as you pass through
>   the middle of the desolated city,
>   like people who seem not to understand
>   the grievous weight of woe it has to bear?
>
> If you would stop to listen to me speak,
>   I know, from what my sighing heart tells me,
>   you would be weeping when you leave this place:
>   lost is the city's source of blessedness,
>   and I know words that could be said of her
>   with power to humble any man to tears.

> *Deh peregrini che pensosi andate,*
>   *forse di cosa che non v'è presente,*
>   *venite voi da sì lontana gente,*
>   *com'a la vista voi ne dimostrate,*
>   *che non piangete quando voi passate*

per lo suo mezzo la città dolente,
come quelle persone che neente
par che 'ntendesser la sua gravitate?

Se voi restaste per volerlo audire,
certo lo cor de' sospiri mi dice
che lagrimando n'uscireste pui.
Ell'ha perduta la sua beatrice;
e le parole ch'om di lei pò dire
hanno vertù di far piangere altrui.

XLI

Some time afterward, two gentlewomen
sent word to me requesting that I send them some of my
poetry. Taking into consideration their noble station, I decided
not only to let them have some of my poems but also to write
something new to go along with those words—in this way doing
their request more honor. So I wrote a sonnet which tells of
my condition and sent it to them accompanied by the preceding
sonnet and by the one which begins: *Now come to me and
listen to my sighs.*

The new sonnet I wrote begins: *Beyond the sphere,* and
contains five parts. In the first I tell where my thought is going,
naming it after one of its effects. In the second I tell why it goes
up there, that is, who causes it to go. In the third I tell what it
saw, that is, a lady being honored up there, and I call it a "pilgrim spirit" because it makes the journey upward spiritually
and, once there, is like a pilgrim far from home. In the fourth
I tell how it sees her to be such, that is of such a nature, that I
cannot understand it: that is to say that my thought ascends
into the nature of this lady to such a degree that my mind
cannot grasp it, for our minds function in relation to those
blessèd souls as the weak eye does in relation to the sun, and
this the Philosopher tells us in the second book of the *Meta-*

physics. In the fifth part I say that, even though I cannot understand what my thought has taken me to see, that is her miraculous nature, at least I understand this much: this thought of mine is entirely about my lady, for many times when it comes to my mind, I hear her name. At the end of this fifth part I say: "dear ladies," so that it be understood that it is to ladies that I speak. The second part begins: *a new intelligence*, the third: *Once arrived*, the fourth: *But when it tries*, the fifth: *This much*. It could be divided and explained more subtly, but since it can pass with this analysis, I do not concern myself with further division.

> Beyond the sphere that makes the widest round,
>   passes the sigh arisen from my heart;
>   a new intelligence that Love in tears
>   endowed it with is urging it on high.
>   Once arrived at the place of its desiring
>   it sees a lady held in reverence,
>   splendid in light; and through her radiance
>   the pilgrim spirit looks upon her being.
>
> But when it tries to tell me what it saw,
>   I cannot understand the subtle words
>   it speaks to the sad heart that makes it speak.
>   I know it tells of that most gracious one,
>   for I often hear the name of Beatrice.
>   This much, at least, is clear to me, dear ladies.

> *Oltre la spera che più larga gira*
>   *passa 'l sospiro ch'esce del mio core:*
>   *intelligenza nova, che l'Amore*
>   *piangendo mette in lui, pur su lo tira.*
>   *Quand'elli è giunto là dove disira,*
>   *vede una donna, che riceve onore,*
>   *e luce sì, che per lo suo splendore*
>   *lo peregrino spirito la mira.*
>
> *Vedela tal, che quando 'l mi ridice,*
>   *io no lo intendo, sì parla sottile*

al cor dolente, che lo fa parlare.
So io che parla di quella gentile,
però che spesso ricorda Beatrice,
sì ch'io lo 'ntendo ben, donne mie care.

XLII

After I wrote this sonnet there came to me a miraculous vision in which I saw things that made me resolve to say no more about this blessèd one until I would be capable of writing about her in a nobler way. To achieve this I am striving as hard as I can, and this she truly knows. Accordingly, if it be the pleasure of Him through whom all things live that my life continue for a few more years, I hope to write of her that which has never been written of any other woman. And then may it please the One who is the Lord of graciousness that my soul ascend to behold the glory of its lady, that is, of that blessèd Beatrice, who in glory contemplates the countenance of the One *qui est per omnia secula benedictus.*[20]

20. ". . . who is through all ages blessed."

Dante's Vita Nuova

An Essay

on the *Vita Nuova*

I *Patterns*

⟨⟨ ⟨⟨ ⟨⟨ ⟨⟨ ⟨⟨ By the end of Chapter II of the *Vita nuova*, that is, by the end of the first chapter of the narrative proper (for the brief Chapter I is only a preface), all of the motifs significant for the story that is about to unfold step by step, have been introduced. The first word of the opening sentence is "Nine":

> "*Nove fiate già appresso lo mio nascimento era tornato lo cielo de la luce quasi a uno medesimo punto, quanto a la sua propia girazione, quando a li miei occhi apparve prima la gloriosa donna de la mia mente, la quale fu chiamata da molti Beatrice li quale non sapeano che si chiamare.*"

> (Nine times already since my birth the heaven of light had circled back to almost the same point, when there appeared before my eyes the now glorious lady of my mind, who was called Beatrice even by those who did not know what her name was.)

The number 9 will be repeated twice more in the next sentence and appears twenty-two times in all within the *Vita nuova*. And not only does the reader find in the first sentence a reference to the number 9 of symbolical significance: he also finds an emphasis on mathematical precision that shows up very frequently throughout Dante's *New Life*. In this same opening sentence the child Beatrice is presented as already enjoying the veneration of the citizens of Florence, including strangers who did not know her name (but who, nevertheless, were inspired to call her Beatrice: ". . . la quale fu chiamata da molti Beatrice li quali non sapeano che si chiamare"). And with the words "la gloriosa donna de la mia mente"—the first of two time-shifts in which the figure of the living Beatrice, at a given moment, is described in such a way as to remind us of Beatrice dead—the theme of death is delicately foreshadowed at the beginning of the story. As for the figure of Beatrice, when she is allowed to be seen for the first time, she is dressed in a garment of blood-red color—the same color as her "shroud" will be in the following chapter. In the next three sentences the three main *spiriti* are introduced: the "vital" (in the heart), the "natural" (in the liver) and the "animal" (in the brain). They rule the body of the nine-year-old protagonist, and they speak in Latin, as will the god of Love in the chapter that follows (and once again later on). The words of the first spirit describing Beatrice, "Ecce deus fortior me, qui veniens *dominabitur* michi" (note the masculine form *deus*), anticipate the first coming of Love, that takes place in the next chapter ("Ego *dominus* tuus"), and suggest something of the same mood of terror. (In this relationship there is contained an implicit suggestion of the parallel between Beatrice and Love which is made explicit in Chapter XXIV.) The words of the second spirit, "Apparuit iam beatitudo vestra," suggest rapturous bliss to come (that bliss rhapsodically described in Chapter XI) while, in the words of the third spirit, there is the first of the many references to tears to be found in the *Vita nuova*. Here it is the spirit of the liver that weeps: "Heu miser, quia frequenter impeditus ero deinceps!" Though this spirit will be mentioned only once again (IV), the reader may gradually come to wonder if the lover's tears, so frequently recorded in the narrative, are not often strongly influenced physiologically.

It is only after this reference to the organ of digestion that Love is mentioned ("D'allora dico che Amore segnoreggiò la mia anima. . ."). He is mentioned first of all as a ruler, but we learn immediately that much of his power is derived from the protagonist's imagination—this faculty of which there will be so many reminders in the form of visions throughout the book. We are also told that Love's power was restricted by reason; later in the book the relation between Love and reason will become a problem. After this summary of the nine years spent by the lover in the service of Beatrice, before she grants him her first greeting (and in this summary is contained the first suggestion of the godlike in Beatrice: "Ella non parea figliuola d'uomo mortale, ma di deo"), the chapter ends with a refusal to go into further details about his youthful behavior (". . . le passioni e atti di tanta gioventudine . . ."). And Chapter II rings throughout with the sound of "praise of the lady," as the protagonist's admiration for Beatrice keeps growing during the nine years after her first appearance.

Thus, this opening chapter prepares for the rest of the book not only in the obvious way of presenting a background situation, an established continuity out of which single events will emerge in time, but also by setting in motion certain forces that will propel the *Vita nuova* forward—forces with which Dante's reader will gradually become more and more familiar.

Of the forty-two chapters of the *Vita nuova* exactly two-thirds contain a poem (two of them contain two poems), a poem which we are expected to believe was inspired by the experience recounted in the prose. The relationship between the experience and the poem may be of two sorts: more than half the time it is the experience itself that is narrated in verse as, for example, in the sonnet describing the first appearance of Love (III); in such cases the effect made by the poem on the reader of the *Vita nuova* is "recapitulative," as if the poem were repeating the prose.[1] The rest of the poems deal not with the experience itself but with ideas suggested and emotions inspired by the experience, as in Chapter VIII when the death of a companion of Beatrice prompts the lover to write two poems about death.

In those poems which simply relate the experience itself this experience is seldom an event in the usual sense. It may be a vision (III, IX, XXIII, XXIV), but more often it is a mood, and usually one in which despondency or tension or both predominate (XIII, XV, XVI, XXXV through XXXIX).[2] Twice, the experience involves an outer event of which the protagonist is an eyewitness. In Chapter XXVI he describes in his two sonnets Beatrice passing before the people, receiving their veneration; he decides to describe this, we learn from the prose narrative, in order that those who cannot see his lady with the physical eye may somehow share the experience from his description. In Chapter XL the outward event described, which also takes place in the streets of the lover's city, has meaning only for himself: he sees a group of pilgrims passing down the middle of the city, having come from other places, on their way to Rome; to his bewilderment they show no signs of grief as they pass through the city widowed by Beatrice's death.

Of the remaining chapters, that is, those in which the theme of the poem is not the event that occasioned its composition, four tell us that the poem represents the fulfillment of a request. The *ballata* of Chapter XII was written at the suggestion of the god of Love; in the other three, the author of the request will be one (or more) of the lover's friends: the admirers of his first *canzone*, who ask him to write a definition of love (XX); the brother of Beatrice who, after her death, indirectly requests a poem about her (XXXII); the two ladies of Chapter XLI who, while they ask the protagonist only to send them some of his already-written poetry, inspire him also to compose a poem especially for them.

Again, the occasion for the poem is the writing of a previous poem. Having written the sonnet of Chapter XX, describing in generic terms the effect on a man of a beautiful woman, the protagonist-lover decides, in Chapter XXI, to continue the theme of love and the gentle heart by limiting the phenomenon of the birth of love to the more extraordinary effect produced by Beatrice. Later, in Chapter XXVII, on re-reading his twin sonnets of praise in Chapter XXVI, that describe the effect of Beatrice on the people of Florence, he finds them defective since nothing was said about her effect on him at the present time. And he begins to write a *canzone* on this theme. The third case in which a poem leads to a poem also involves disappointment over the previous composition: having written in Chapter XXXIII a poem for Beatrice's brother, the lover decides in the next chapter that the close relationship between brother and sister calls for a worthier poem, and he writes a *canzone* of two stanzas.

It could be said that in all three cases it is the protagonist's thoughts rather than some outward event that provides the occasion for writing the poems. And this is all that can be said of the inspiration of the poem in Chapter XXXIV. On the anniversary of Beatrice's death the lover sits remembering her and drawing the figure of an angel on "certe tavolette." He looks up to see a group of men watching him, and speaks the ambiguous words, "Altri era testè meco, però pensava." After their departure he returns to his sketching, in the midst of which he decides to write an anniversary poem—which, we can only assume, continues the thoughts that came to him as the angel took form under his hand.

With the rest of the poems the occasion is a happening which takes place in society. In Chapter VII, after his first screen-lady has left Florence for a far-away place, the protagonist decides to write a poem expressing grief over her departure. One might call the theme of his poem "loss of a loved one." And in Chapter VIII this theme is found again, in a tragic sense: both poems in this chapter are poems of mourning for the death of a lovely young lady who had been one of Beatrice's companions. There will be three more poems of mourning: two in Chapter XXII, occasioned by the death of Beatrice's father, and in Chapter XXXI, the last *canzone*, in which the dead Beatrice is mourned.

In addition to the theme of death (loss) there is the theme of mockery. Already in Chapter IV the ravaged appearance of the young lover (whose absorption in Beatrice had been detrimental to his *spirito naturale*) had aroused the impertinent curiosity of his neighbors. In Chapter XIV the suggestion of mockery introduced earlier takes the form of a public humiliation. Having accompanied a friend of his to a wedding feast where Beatrice is present, the lover collapses at the sight of her; his appearance provokes the derision of the ladies surrounding Beatrice and he sees her laughing with them. The chapter ends with a sonnet written to his lady, reproaching her for her cruelty and appealing to her pity by describing in detail the disastrous effects of her presence on his nervous system. And there are reverberations of this scene of mockery in the two chapters that follow; the lover, still suffering from the shameful memory and wrestling with the problems it raises, writes two more sonnets in which he mainly seeks to explain to his lady the paradoxical effect her desired presence produces in him—making of him the object of her mockery.

The importance of the theme of death, which culminates in the central *canzone* and lingers to the end, hardly needs to be stressed; as all readers of the *Vita nuova* know, it is central to an understanding of the work. The theme of mockery does not seem to have attracted the attention of the critics; but as we shall see later, in the final part of this essay, the theme of mockery is also central, and it works on more than one level. The one instance of mockery discussed so far (and there will be a similar scene later on), has been simply society's punishment for the young lover's foolishness and morbidity.

The prose that relates the events offers a narrative that is remarkably objective. Never does the author pause to reprove or commend the protagonist; even the descriptions of his emotions are done in a rather detached way. But not always is the author content to be the simple narrator of past events; occasionally the reader hears the author's voice speaking on a time-level different from that of the narrative. Sometimes, when we hear his voice, the effect is merely that of a tilting upward of the time level, as when he describes Beatrice in her lifetime in such a way as to remind us of her death (in fact, she is introduced to the reader in terms that could apply only to Beatrice dead). More directly, as if in a conversation with his reader, he may explicitly contrast the present with the past: he tells us (III) that the significance of his first sonnet, which no one perceived at the time the poem was written and circulated, is "now" apparent to the least sophisticated. Much more often, however, we are also made aware of Dante's concerns as author of the *Vita nuova:* we not only hear him speak on the post-narrative plane, we see him sitting at his desk. In fact, that is precisely where he is when the *Vita nuova* opens, for it opens with a proem announcing his intentions. Later we see him adding many things to the factual details of the narrative, the most consistent pattern of such "glosses" being that of the *divisioni* which the author felt necessary to add to most of the poems he includes in his work. Then there are the "essays" represented by Chapter XXV and XXIX in which he treats, respectively, the use of poetic license and the significance of the number 9—and the two brief interpolations in Chapters XXII and XL, the first concerned with the bond that unites a good father and a good child, the second with the terminology appropriate for the various types of pilgrims according to their geographical goals.

As for Dante's device of *divisioni*, which were omitted by Boccaccio in his edition of the *Vita nuova*, and which most readers since then have found tedious and unrewarding, how is his predilection for such analysis to be explained? The *divisioni* never serve to clear up any difficult points the poem may contain; they do serve, as he himself claims in Chapter XIV, to "open up" (*aprire*) the poem, but the parts into which it is neatly dissected are almost always obviously given, like the wedges of an orange. It is not enough to compare Dante's procedure here with the common practice of the Scholastics—for example, Aquinas' commentaries on Aristotle with their divisions and subdivisions of the original text. In the first place we have, with Aquinas, one writer commenting on another (and a Christian on a Pagan); secondly, the work which Aquinas divides with his prose headings was itself prose. Dante is the first to have applied this scholastic procedure to poetry. He will use this device again in the *Convivio*, but there it serves a necessary function: it would be impossible for the reader to follow the lengthy allegorical interpretations of the poems without having the poetic material first cut into pieces for him (as a father cuts his child's meat for him at the table). But there are few interpretations, allegorical or otherwise, contained in the *divisioni* in the *Vita nuova*.[3]

I wonder if, in this work, Dante was not interested in the abstract act of subdividing for subdividing's sake, and if he might not have had an artistic interest in breaking down a poetic structure into conceptual units. Any poem with fixed rhyme and meter, particularly a sonnet, already offers a rigid system of subdivisions; in breaking this down into conceptual units one is dissecting an artistic compound of a certain tangible form into parts not necessarily given by that form. And a number of the poems in the *Vita nuova* for which *divisioni* are offered show a conceptual pattern at variance with the metric pattern, to a greater or lesser degree: Chapters IX, XII, XIII, XXI, XXIII, XXIV, XXXII, XXXVII, XLI.[4]

In presenting the third and last *canzone* of the *Vita nuova* Dante changes the position of the *divisioni,* letting them now precede the poem instead of follow it. He does this, he says, in order that the *canzone* may seem to remain more "widowed" after it has come to an end: "—Acciò che questa canzone paia rimanere più vedova dopo lo suo fine. . . ." He will continue to follow this order with the rest of the poems. The reader may wonder why Dante's artistic instinct had not shown him earlier that the poetic effect of a lyrical composition should be allowed to linger on; to follow the poem immediately by a rational analysis of its parts must tend to kill the effect. But I shall treat this matter later in this essay.

Behind Dante's fondness for his *divisioni* may also be his delight in mathematical figures and procedures. What comes to mind immediately is the importance he gives to the number 9 throughout the work and, in Chapter XXIX, his fascination with its divisibility, yielding three as the square root. And one remembers his use of the figure of the circle with its center equidistant from all points on the circumference (XII). There are also indications of his interest in geometrical form that show no concern with symbolical interpretation—for instance, the description of the passage of the pilgrims along a street "la quale è quasi mezzo de la cittade ove nacque e vivette e morìo la gentilissima donna" (XL). This city, which incidentally, the reader is never permitted to visualize, can be, like any other geometrical form, divided into two equal parts. There is a similar, and most effective indication of his interest in sheer geometrical form in Chapter V, where he describes the circumstances that led to the choice of the first screen-lady:

Uno giorno avvenne che questa gentilissima sedea in parte
ove s'udiano parole de la regina de la gloria, ed io era in
luogo dal quale vedea la mia beatitudine; e nel mezzo di lei
e di me per la retta linea *sedea una gentile donna di molto*
piacevole aspetto, la quale mi mirava spesse volte, maravigli-
andosi del mio squardare, che parea che sopra lei terminasse.
Onde molti s'accorsero de lo suo mirare; e in tanto vi fue
posto mente, che, partendomi da questo luogo, mi sentìo
dicere appresso di me: "Vedi come cotale donna distrugge la
persona de costui"; e nominandola, io intesi che dicea di colei
che mezzo era stata ne la linea retta *che movea da la genti-*
lissima Beatrice e terminava ne li occhi miei.

(It happened one day that this most gracious of ladies was
sitting in a place where words about the Queen of Glory
were being spoken, and I was in a place where I could
behold my bliss. *Halfway between her and me, in a direct*
line of vision, sat a gentlewoman of a very pleasing appearance, who glanced at me frequently as if bewildered by my
gaze, which appeared to be directed at her. And many began to notice her glances in my direction, and paid close
attention to them and, as I left this place, I heard someone
near me say: "See what a devastating effect that lady has
had on that man." And, when her name was mentioned, I
realized that the lady referred to was the one *whose place*
had been half way along the direct line which extended
from the most gracious Beatrice, ending in my eyes.)

So the lady was exactly in the middle of the direct line of
vision extending from the lover to the Belovèd! The lover
must have had a feeling of fatality. Suddenly there were only
three persons in the church, there were only three points on
the line. And twice the idea is stressed of a straight line intersected in the middle.

There is further evidence of this mathematical interest to be
deduced from the symmetrical distribution of the three *can-*
zoni. The first *canzone* is preceded by ten poems, the last is
followed by ten poems, and on each side of the central *canzone*
are four poems giving the schema (the *canzoni* being indicated

by Roman numerals): 10 /I / 4 / II / 4 / III / 10. More-over, the central grouping containing the mid-*canzone* offers a section of nine poems; thus, disregarding the distinction between *canzone* and non-*canzone*, we find the undifferentiated schema: 10 / 1 / 9 / 1 / 10.[5] Surely the first distribution, with its three symmetrically-placed *canzoni*, was deliberately intended by the poet; and the same is probably true for the second with its central 9.

The discussion of Dante's mathematical thinking was offered as an explanation of the poet's particular device of *divisioni*, the most ambitious of his techniques as "glossator"—that is, as one who makes additions to the factual details of the narrative. But not only does Dante make additions, there are also omissions of what might have been written down (it could perhaps be said that Dante the poet serves to "edit" as well as to "gloss"). Usually, when he confesses an omission he explains his motive; thus, he refuses to discuss in any detail the first nine years of his love for Beatrice (II), because of his immaturity at the time. Much more significant is his refusal to describe the death of Beatrice; for it he offers a three-fold motivation (XXVIII). Several times he announces that he will withhold from us certain of his literary compositions, the writing of which was described in the narrative.[6]

In his Proem to the *Vita nuova*, where he presents himself as a scribe copying from his "Book of Memory," Dante nevertheless makes allowances for omissions of factual detail, when a reference to the significance of an event seems sufficient (he says nothing, however, of his plans to make additions to the events, in the form of glosses or otherwise):[7]

> *In quella parte del libro de la mia memoria dinanzi a la quale poco si potrebbe leggere, si trova una rubrica la quale dice:* Incipit vita nova. *Sotto la quale rubrica io trovo scritte le parole le quali è mio intendimento d'assemplare in questo libello,* e se non tutte, almeno la loro sentenza.

(In The Book of Memory, in the early part where there is little to be read, there comes a chapter with the rubric: *Incipit vita nuova*. It is my intention to copy into this little book the words I find written under that heading, *if not all of them, at least the essence of their meaning.*)

Now in Chapter XXVII, when refusing to discuss the death of Beatrice, Dante offers as his first justification the terms of the Proem (the only time in the book that he sends us back to his preface), and it must have been precisely the final words which I have italicized above that he had in mind. It was the significance of Beatrice's death that alone mattered, and this significance had already been made evident in Chapter XXIII containing his prophetic vision of her death. What more could be added to the magnificent and terrible picture there offered?[8] (It is also natural for the young lover to decide at this point, when faced with the simple, sheer fact of his lady's death, to be silent and shun rhetoric of his own.) And obviously, these final words of his Proem explain his much less dramatic silence as to the many events that must have taken place in the time-span included in Chapter II. One may also think of Chapter V in which the events of several years are summed up.

But perhaps the final words of the Proem in which Dante claims the right to omit reference to unessential details, cover even more than has been assumed so far. Perhaps they serve, somehow, to explain the shadowy, impalpable world in which the lover seems to move. What does that world contain? There are exactly two references to concrete objects (both times the noun is subordinated by a preposition): the bed on which the lover lies during the illness that produced his prophetic vision of Beatrice's death, and the "certe tavolette" on which he was drawing figures of angels on the anniversary of Beatrice's death—probably the same angels he had seen in his macabre vision. As for places, twice the lover is represented as being out-of-doors in Nature: in Chapters IX and XIX (in both scenes only one detail is described and it is the same detail in each: a very clear stream flowing by the side of his path).

Not once is a building described, and only once are we offered a descriptive detail of an interior: the frescoed wall against which the lover was forced to lean for support, having sensed the presence of Beatrice at the wedding feast. We are never given a glimpse of the city of Florence. Its massive medieval architecture has dissolved; its twisted, busy, colorful streets have been reduced to straight lines in space, along which Beatrice or a group of pilgrims passes—the one to receive the worship of the crowds we do not see, the others on their way to worship at a far-off shrine.

Not only is there a dearth of descriptive detail, occasionally we have no idea where we are. One of the liveliest scenes in the *Vita nuova* is that of Chapter XVIII, when the lover explains to a group of ladies gathered together the new source of happiness he has found, and listens with some shame to the reactions of one of them. But where are these ladies who listen so attentively? Are they outdoors against a backdrop of Nature (they can hardly be on the street), or are they in some Florentine home (like the groups in Chapters VIII and XIV)? Probably we are meant to think of them as being outdoors, given the author's words "e io passando appresso da loro."[9] And perhaps the same should be deduced for Chapter XXXIV: the lover, surrounded by a group of men who have come uninvited, must have been somewhere outdoors; but we are told only that he was in a place where he was drawing an angel and thinking of Beatrice. In the relative clause, "in parte ne la quale ricordandomi di lei, disegnavo uno angelo . . . ," it is as though the activity that he was in the midst of constituted a place.

If Dante has cut out the sensuous details of his environment, all but obliterating the physical world, it must be because this world had no significance for his story. It is also true that, by this negative approach, he has achieved something positive, a suggestion of universality: this city in which a moral drama was unfolding could be any city belonging to any time (and the lover could be any man, or Everyman). In fact, the name of the city, the beautiful evocative name, Firenze, is never mentioned.

As for people who inhabit this nowhere place, the author's treatment of them is appropriately vague. He never mentions the members of his family with whom he must be living, except for the "donna giovane e gentile" in Chapter XXIII sitting by his bed of delirium, who must have been his sister—as we learn only after she has been sent from the room. (She goes out of the room trailing behind her a relative clause of identification: ". . . facendo lei partire da me, *la quale era meco di propinquissima sanguinitade congiunta.*") In the case of Beatrice's family we learn only after his death that she had a father. In Chapter XXXII her brother comes into existence in order to make a literary request of the lover, and turns out to be Dante's closest friend after Cavalcanti.

None of these three persons is even minimally described; there is the same lack of sensory detail in the presentation of characters as in that of places. And this is extraordinary if we think of Chrétien de Troyes before Dante and of Boccaccio soon after him—and of Dante himself as author of the *Divine Comedy* with its richly sensuous descriptions. Never is a character presented as a figure of flesh and blood in Dante's *Vita nuova*, even though by his time, and long before, the art of verbal portraiture had been extensively developed. In fact, of the five single individuals who are brought on stage at a given moment—the protagonist's sister, the "amica persona" who takes him to the wedding feast, Beatrice, the first screen-lady and the lady at the window—only the last three receive even minimal description. Beatrice first appears wearing a crimson robe, girdled and trimmed as it should have been ("a la guisa che a la sua giovanissima etade si convenia"); next she appears in purest white. The red of *caritas*, the white of purity! She is the only one whose clothing is described, and after these two appearances her garments are never again mentioned (except in the visions); in fact, according to the opening words of the first description, Beatrice is not dressed in a garment, she is dressed in a color. And Beatrice does not have a face in the prose narrative of the *Vita nuova*, as do the other two ladies. The one sitting in church between the young lover and Beatrice was "di molto piacevole aspetto," and the young lady at the window is described as very beautiful and pale of color, with an expression of great compassion. That Beatrice's garments alone are described is due to their symbolic significance, and not only the obvious significance of the two colors, red and white: she wears her virtues as a garment, as the poet will tell his reader later, in a sonnet: "Benignamente d'umiltà vestuta." And if the two other ladies are described in terms of personal physical charm, the meaning of the difference should be obvious.

The other characters that cross the bare stage of the *Vita nuova* appear in groups, from the pair of older ladies walking on either side of Beatrice, to the masses of Florentine people who flock to see the lady Beatrice pass.[10] As the groups appear, the narrator points to them: "molti," "altri," "molte donne," "alcune donne," "certe donne," "uomini," "alquanti peregrini."

Strikingly different from these colorless, nonindividualizing phrases are those periphrases, equally abstract and nonindividualizing, which offer, however, an essence: the sister of the protagonist and the father and brother of Beatrice, brought so suddenly into existence from nowhere, are presented not by means of the normal words *padre*, *fratello*, *sorella*, with their overtones of warmth, but by analytical designations of relationship. Beatrice's father is called "colui che era stato genitore di tanta maraviglia quanta si vedea ch'era questa nobilissima Beatrice";[11] Beatrice's brother and the protagonist's sister are presented in terms of degree of consanguinity: the former as "tanto distretto di sanguinitade con questa gloriosa, che nullo più presso l'era," the latter as being "meco di propinquissima sanguinitade congiunta."

The same device of significant periphrases is used of places: a minor case is that of the church in which the main event of Chapter V takes place. Not only is the church left undescribed but it is not even called a church: in the opening sentence Beatrice is presented as sitting "in parte ove s'udiano parole de la regina de la gloria." On a larger scale this device is used, and most effectively, in connection with the city of Florence. The first reference to Dante's birthplace occurs in Chapter VI which contains the apparently insignificant reference to the composition of a *serventese* including sixty names of beautiful ladies: ". . . e presi li nomi de sessanta le più belle donne de *la cittade ove la mia donna fue posta da l'altissimo sire.*" In the following chapter Florence is referred to as "la sopradetta cittade". And in the next six references the same deictic phrase is found: seven echoes, that is, of the first periphrasis that was meant to remind the reader of Beatrice and of her destiny and role in this story. In Chapter XL we read that "alquanti peregrini passavano per una via la quale è quazi mezzo de la *cittade ove nacque e vivette e morìo la gentilissima donna.*" This city has now become the place where Beatrice also died. Thus, in Dante's treatment of the city of Florence there are two forces at work: on the one hand, in the interest of universality, suppression of all picturesque detail, suppression even of the name itself which might evoke such detail; on the other, the formulation of a periphrasis that offers the true significance of that city for the lover (and therefore for the reader).

It seems clear that Dante's desire to create for his reader a world in which concrete detail has been reduced to a minimum, a shadowy nameless city peopled by nameless shadows, has some connection with his predilection for mathematical forms and processes. There are times, when places are in question, that the two tendencies coincide: the street along which the pilgrims move, and which the reader is not invited to visualize, is presented as dissecting the city of Florence in two; the house of worship that cannot be seen contains a straight line intersected by three points. This extreme concern with the abstract implies an extreme concern for the spiritual, which means a concern for the essential—which is precisely what Dante was revealing in the last words of the *Proemio:* ". . . se non tutte, almeno la loro sentenzia."

Perhaps the most effective example of such concerns is to be found in the scene describing Beatrice's greeting. That event which occurred nine years to the day after the lover's first sight of her, that event without which what does happen could never have happened—takes place in no particular place:

> *Avvenne che questa mirabile donna apparve a me vestita di colore bianchissimo . . . ; e passando per una via, volse li occhi verso quella parte ov' io era molto pauroso, e per la sua ineffabile cortesia, la quale è oggi meritata nel grande secolo, mi salutoe molto virtuosamente tanto che me parve allora vedere tutti li termini de la beatitudine.*

> (It happened that, on the last one of those days, the miraculous lady appeared dressed in purest white . . . ; *and passing along a certain street,* she turned her eyes to where I was standing faint-hearted and, with that indescribable graciousness for which today she is rewarded in the eternal life, she greeted me so marvelously that I seemed at that moment to behold the entire range of possible bliss.)

But what does it matter exactly where Beatrice was that day? What matters is that she is now in Heaven. And the reference to her "indescribable graciousness," which would seem to lead directly to the announcement of her greeting, is instead followed by a reminder of Beatrice in glory: in the split-second interval between the moment she turns her eyes and the moment of her greeting, we catch a glimpse of Heaven. Also in the description of Beatrice's first appearance on stage the reader had been reminded of her death by the simple device of using an epithet applicable only to her role after death; the effect was completely static. Here, however, there is movement, and interruption of movement, and movement again: Beatrice alive, Beatrice dead, Beatrice continuing to live.

As the reader will surely remember, there is much more vitality, movement, color in the narration of the visions than in that of the events of the real world of the *Vita nuova*.[12] The most vivid of the visions are those contained in Chapters III and XXIII, both of them prophetic of Beatrice's death, the first more touched with mystery, the second characterized by more phantasmagoric elements. Thus, the poet does not hesitate to appeal to the senses of his reader when describing a visionary world; and if Dante's descriptions throughout the *Divine Comedy* show a colorful technique so at variance with the shadowy outlines of the *Vita nuova* as a whole, this must be because the *Divine Comedy* is, throughout, one continuous vision. Hell, Purgatory, and Paradise and the souls that are hopelessly damned, or suffering in hope, or enjoying the beatific vision in those three realms, respectively, are described in greater detail because, being eternal, they are more real than are this world and the souls that temporarily inhabit it. The visions, too, in the *Vita nuova* are more real than any one of the events in the story proper, for there, as we shall soon see, the protagonist is offered glimpses of eternity.

II   *Aspects*

All of the characters in the *Vita nuova* were mentioned in the preceding chapter of this essay, with the important exception of one of the three main characters in this love-story: the god of Love, who appears on stage playing an important role in Chapters III, IX, XXI and XXIV. In most of his visits to the lover this being is presented far more vividly than any of the other characters seen by the protagonist—who, for the most part, come through to the reader as shadowy shapes indeed. The first three times Love makes his entrance onto the stage of the *Vita nuova*, not only are his clothes described but also his gestures and movements; and in all four of his appearances Love's voice is heard.[1] This character, on whom a spotlight is focused, is made to behave in a way that must puzzle any reader. Love speaks Italian sometimes, sometimes Latin, and sometimes he even shifts languages in the midst of a visit. The accouterments of this actor in the scenes in which he plays his different roles vary, being those of a terrifying deity, a shabby traveler or a guardian angel. And so do his moods change, not only from scene to scene but within the same scene: from the radiant happiness of majesty, or the poised tranquility of beatitude, Love will fall into bitter weeping. Or, again, in his relationship toward the lover he may shift from kindly counselor to sublimely haughty lord, to impatient monitor, to chatty conspiratorial advisor. What can be the true significance of this mysterious, protean figure of Love, who four times appears on stage at a given moment to address the lover?[2]

The god of Love first appears to the lover on the evening after he has received Beatrice's first greeting and returned home, ecstatic, to fall into a sweet sleep (III). He dreams he sees Love holding a sleeping lady in his arms; the figure speaks to the lover, in Latin, words that are mainly incomprehensible, and then ascends to Heaven. In Chapter IX the protagonist sees the figure of Love walking toward him along a country road; Love offers him practical advice as to maintaining the stratagem of the screen-lady. In Chapter XII, just as in Chapter III, Love appears to him during his sleep, a sleep into which he has fallen grieving bitterly over the loss of his lady's greeting. In Chapter XXIV, which immediately follows the prophetic vision of Beatrice's death, the lover is sitting thoughtful in "a certain place" when he sees Love coming from the direction "where his lady was." Then Beatrice appears with another lady, and he listens to Love's comments about them.

Now this last vision is followed by an "essay" (XXV) which begins with an explanation of the author's treatment of Love; though he mentions only the scene in Chapter XXIV, his words are surely meant to apply to all of the appearances of Love. But anyone familiar with the *Vita nuova*, who is interested in the significance of the figure of Love, knows that in this chapter he will find no clue to the proper interpretation of this mysterious figure. The chapter treats instead the problem of poetic license, involving particularly the device of personification (a treatment promised us somewhat cryptically in Chapter XII). And it is puzzling that precisely after the last appearance of Love Dante would refer to this figure for no other reason than a rhetorical one. Perhaps there is a more important purpose underyling this chapter, whose threefold structure can be briefly summed up.

First, he admits that, while perfectly aware of Love's being only an accident in a substance, he has treated it as if it were a substance—in fact, he has attributed to the figure of Love qualities properly human. Rather abruptly he turns to a consideration of the recent phenomenon of poets writing in the vernacular, stating that they should be allowed poetic license equal to that of the poets of antiquity: in particular, the animization or personification of abstract entities. (Curious, that of the many poetic figures recognized by medieval rhetoric, Dante specifies only the concretization of the abstract.) Finally, he illustrates the poetic license in question with quotations from the classical poets.

But he concludes the second part by allowing this poetic license to the vernacular poet only on one condition:

> . . . degno è lo dicitore per rima di fare lo somigliante, ma non sanza ragione alcuna, ma con ragione la quale poi sia possibile d'aprire per prosa.

> (. . . it is fitting that the vernacular poet do the same—not, of course, without some reason, but with a motive that later can be explained in prose.)[3]

And he repeats this warning toward the end of the chapter:

> Però che grande vergogna sarebbe a colui che rimasse cose sotto vesta di figura o di colore rettorico, e poscia, domandato, non sapesse denudare le sue parole da cotale vesta, in guisa che avessero verace intendimento.

> (For, if any one should dress his poem in images and rhetorical coloring and then, being asked to strip his poem of such dress in order to reveal its true meaning, would not be able to do so—this would be a veritable cause for shame.)

This warning by the author amounts to a claim that he himself would be capable of offering the "verace intendimento" of the figure of Love, if asked to do so. To the reader who cannot ask the author to do so, these words are frustrating. But I believe they were intended to serve as a challenge to the reader, to inspire in him confidence that the device exploited is not mere ornamentation (as is the case, so the author tells us, with some poets known to him and Cavalcanti): there is indeed a "verace intendimento" which could be unmysteriously explained, and knowing this, the reader of the *Vita nuova* must try, and hope, to find it. And perhaps the author is also suggesting—this would be most important—that because this significance can be ultimately made clear, no detail of his figurative presentation should be overlooked.[4]

Of the four visions the first I find the most difficult; the simplest is the last, and with this I shall begin.[5] In Chapter XXIV the first words of Love are a joyful command to the lover that he bless the day he became Love's captive, whereupon the lover, too, is filled with joy. Then he sees the "miraculous Beatrice" coming toward him, preceded by her friend Giovanna, called also Primavera. He hears Love speak portentous words comparing the Lady Giovanna, who comes before Beatrice, with John the Baptist proclaiming the approach of Christ. Love ends by saying: "E chi volesse sottilmente considerare, quella Beatrice chiamarebbe Amor per molta simiglianza che ha meco." ("Anyone of subtle discernment would call Beatrice Love, because she so greatly resembles me.") Thus, Love is comparing Beatrice indirectly to Christ and directly to himself.

We can surely assume, whatever the special significance we attribute to the figure of Love that, in each of the four visions in question, he always represents in some way the protagonist's love for Beatrice. And I suggest that here he represents the lover's total potential capacity for loving Beatrice as she should be loved: recognizing her Christlike nature which can only be unselfishly adored. This figure, which may be called by the formula "The Greater Aspect" of Dante's love for Beatrice, we shall see again as we go back to the other visions in the *Vita nuova*.

But if we turn next to the other *imaginazione* (IX) among the four scenes, we will find the sharpest of contrasts. The lover himself is in a mood of dejection since he is forced to undertake a journey away from his city and from his lady; and the figure he suddenly sees coming toward him has the form of a pilgrim lightly and poorly clad—he, too, seeming dejected, staring at the ground, occasionally turning his glance toward a beautiful stream, swift and very clear, which flows alongside the path he is traveling. He advises the lover to choose a new screen-lady since the first one has left the city, and he urges him to be as ardently adept in his dissimulation with the second lady as he has been with the first. Surely this figure can only represent the "Lesser Aspect" of the protagonist's love, the lover's feelings at the moment, which are untouched by the transcendental. The lover's emotional state is reflected in the epithet "disbigottito" applied to Love—who appears dressed as a pilgrim, since the lover himself happens to be a pilgrim at the present moment. Moreover, Love is poorly dressed; with this latter detail it is as if the poet would symbolize in Love's outward appearance the inner misery he himself is experiencing. And we learn that Love is playing the role of the lover's accomplice in the foolish game of the screen-ladies. The advice he offers, of a practical, even cynical nature, is of the sort to appeal to the childishly scheming lover.

There are two other indications that the Love who figures in this scene is none other than a reflection of the protagonist's own limited feelings: one concerned with Love's entrance on stage, the other with his disappearance. Love disappears, not as a person, not as a figure disappears, but as a substance melts. There is nothing left of Love for the lover to see, we are told, because Love has become so much a part of him. The manner of his appearance or, rather, the reason for his appearance also is connected with his being a part of the lover: after speaking of his anguish at leaving Florence and Beatrice, the lover adds, as if it were the most natural thing imaginable: "e *però* lo dolcissimo segnore . . . ne la mia imaginazione apparve come pellegrino. . . ." The significance of the causal *però* is obvious: it was the intensity of his feelings that caused his love to take on form and shape, reflecting his own mood, before his eyes.

In Chapter XII Love appears to the protagonist in his sleep; he sees Love sitting near his bed dressed in the whitest of raiment, deep in thought. After looking for some time at the lover, the figure sighs and says "Fili mi, tempus est ut pretermictantur simulacra nostra" ("My son, it is time to do away with our false ideals"). The lover notes that Love is weeping, and senses that he is waiting for him to say something. He can only ask: "Segnore della nobilitade, e perché piangi tu?" ("Lord of all virtues, why do you weep?"). He hears the answer:

> *"Ego tanquam centrum circuli, cui simili modo se habent circumferentie partes; tu autem non sic."*

> ("I am like the center of a circle, equidistant from all points on the circumference; you, however, are not.")

Finding these words obscure, the lover gathers courage to ask Love to explain them. Love answers, this time in Italian: "Non dimandare più che utile ti sia" ("Do not ask more than is useful to you").

The figure of the young man sitting dressed in purest white will remind any reader of the young man dressed in a long white garment sitting at the door of Christ's sepulchre. This suggestion, together with the solemnity of his Latin words, can only mean that, of the two Aspects of Love already discussed, the figure now on the stage of the lover's mind represents the Greater Aspect, that transcends the lover's own feelings on this occasion. And Love's first words of tender reproach are those of a father to a son.

Most critics have seen in Love's first words announcing the necessity of abandoning *"simulacra nostra"* a reference to the device of the screen-ladies; and to them the possessive pronoun *nostra* amounts to a confession of complicity on the part of Love, who had encouraged the protagonist to continue this device. But it is surely impossible to imagine that the noble figure here portrayed could ever have played this puerile role; it is not he but the shabbily dressed pilgrim figure of Chapter IX, the Lesser Aspect, who had done so. And to imagine that this aider-and-abettor of the lover's game of screen-ladies would suddenly appear like an angel and, addressing him as "Fili mi", confess that they had both been wrong to play this game, is absurd. As for the possessive adjective *nostra* I see in this not a true plural but the well-known pedagogic device ("Fili mi") recorded from antiquity, of replacing the second person singular by the first person plural as if to include the speaker along with the person addressed, the teacher with the pupil. This is a sympathetic and a patronizing device. Thus, assuming that *simulacra* is an illusion to the screen-ladies, the Greater Aspect would be here reproaching the lover for his weakness (that the Lesser Aspect had encouraged).

But I do not believe that the word *simulacra* refers specifically to the lover's use of screen-ladies, though such an allusion may well be included within the referential range of this word. In classical Latin the word *simulacrum*, in its philosophical application, was used of an imitation as opposed to the original, of an appearance as opposed to what is real. Thus, it could apply to any of the attitudes or actions of the young lover which were only false imitations of what true love for Beatrice should be. And if Love uses the word *simulacra* at this moment of the lover's development, while he is plunged in grief because of the loss of Beatrice's greeting, he must intend it to be a condemnation, particularly, of the superficiality of a love that would seek its happiness in something transient, in a reward that could be arbitrarily bestowed or withdrawn. The greeting of Beatrice had seemed to the young lover to represent the ultimate in bliss ("mi *parve* allora vedere tutti li termini de la beatitudine"), but it was only a seeming, a *simulacrum*. Thus, Love's first words would seek to teach the lover, mourning the destruction of his happiness, the vanity of that happiness itself.

At this point one could hardly expect on the part of the protagonist immediate understanding of the rebuke, and immediate agreement with Love's suggestion. It would not be unreasonable, however, to expect at least a desire to understand: the lover might have asked his lord to explain what was implied by the word *simulacra* so that he should know just what it was he should avoid. But if we read carefully from the beginning of the vision, it would seem as if he has not heard the words of admonition:

> *Avvenne quasi nel mezzo de lo mio dormire che me parve vedere ne la mia camera lungo me sedere uno giovane vestito di bianchissime vestimenta, e pensando molto quanto a la vista sua, mi riguardava là ov'io giacea; e quando m'avea guardato alquanto, pareami che sospirando mi chiamasse, e diceami queste parole: "Fili mi, tempus est ut pretermictantur simulacra nostra." Allora mi parea che io lo conoscesse, però che mi chiamava così come assai fiate ne li miei sonni m'avea già chiamato; e riguardandolo, parvemi che piangesse pietosamente, e parea che attendesse da me alcuna parola; ond'io, assicurandomi, cominciai a parlare così con esso: "Segnore de la nobiltade, e perché piangi tu?"*

(About half-way through my sleep I seemed to see in my room a young man sitting near the bed dressed in the whitest of garments and, from his expression, he seemed to be deep in thought, watching me where I lay; after looking at me for some time, he seemed to sigh and to call to me, saying these words: *Fili mi, tempus est ut pretermictantur simulacra nostra* ("My son, it is time to do away with our false ideals.") Then I seemed to know who he was, for he was calling me in the same way that many times before in my sleep he had called me; and as I watched him, it seemed to me that he was weeping piteously, and he seemed to be waiting for me to say something to him; so, gathering courage, I began to address him, saying: "Lord of all virtues, why do you weep?")

The lover has heard the first two words, of course: "Fili mi", for they have served to make him recognize his lord. (Thus, between the vision in Chapter III and this one, there must have been other times when Love appeared to the sleeping lover, addressing him in paternal terms.) He also notes that Love, silent again, is weeping and seems to be waiting for him to speak. And thus encouraged, he speaks—but, for some strange reason, only to inquire about Love's tears, not to comment on Love's message, his words of admonition, as would seem to be the normal thing to do. According to what we are offered of the protagonist's thought processes, he must have taken in only the first two words, missing the message itself: "Tempus est ut. . . ." Once he was sure that it was Love speaking, his attention passed from Love's words to his tears and to his waiting attitude, and he evidently believed that his puerile question was what Love was waiting to hear. But, of course, if he had understood Love's admonition, he would not have needed to ask him why he wept.

Love weeps because of the *simulacra*. Love weeps because the lover had put an exaggerated value on a mere greeting.[6] He also weeps because, once this was refused, the lover collapsed utterly and childishly, instead of learning from this experience the obvious lesson—which he was to learn only later, thanks to his Muse (XVIII). If the lover did not understand the reason for Love's tears, little wonder that he did not understand Love's enigmatic answer, "Ego tanquam centrum circuli . . ."—words which have baffled generations of critics of the *Vita nuova*.

As for the interpretation of these words that the lover did not understand, surely, given the context, the comparison they offer between Love and the young lover is a comparison between the two kinds of Love that must be distinguished: the lover's love, though tending toward the center is still on the circumference of the circle (where the *simulacra* are), while Love, the Greater Love, is, was, and always will be the irradiating center. And not only has Love, with his geometrical metaphor, set the *simulacra* in perspective, he has, in his self-definition, revealed his divine nature: in defining himself he uses a common Patristic definition of God.[7] (And the *Paradise* will end with the adoration of the perfection of the circle, to the movement of the three circles that are the Trinity and therefore the One.)

After the lover has been told not to ask more about what he obviously does not understand ("Non dimandare più che utile ti sia") he starts talking about himself. He laments the loss of Beatrice's greeting and asks for an explanation of it. Love tells him that Beatrice's rejection was due to the scandalous rumors about his relationship with the second screen-lady. He then proceeds to offer the lover a means of ingratiating himself with Beatrice once more, describing in some detail the kind of poem he should write her, one which would implore her forgiveness and appeal to Love himself as a witness to his loyalty:

> *Onde, con ciò sia cosa che veracemente sia conosciuto per lei alquanto lo tuo secreto per lunga consuetudine, voglio che tu dichi certe parole per rima ne le quali tu comprendi la forza che io tegno sopra te per lei, e come tu fosti suo tostamente da la tua puerizia; e di ciò chiama testimonio colui che lo sa, e come tu prieghi lui che li le dica: ed io, che son quelli, volentieri le ne ragionerò; e per questo sentirà ella la tua volontade, la quale sentendo, conoscerà le parole de li ingannati. Queste parole fa che siano quasi un mezzo, sì che tu non parli a lei immediatamente, che non è degno; e no le mandare in parte, sanza me ove potessero essere intese da lei, ma falle adornare di soave armonia, ne la quale io sarò tutte le volte che farà mestiere." E dette queste parole, sì disparve, e lo mio sonno fue rotto.*

(Since she has really been more or less aware of your secret for quite some time, I want you to write a certain poem, in which you make clear the power I have over you through her, explaining that ever since you were a boy you have belonged to her; and, concerning this, call as witness him who knows, and say that you are begging him to testify on your behalf; and I, who am that witness, will gladly explain it to her, and from this she will understand your true feelings and, understanding them, she will also set the proper value on the words of those people who were mistaken. Let your words themselves be, as it were, an intermediary, whereby you will not be speaking directly to her, for this would not be fitting; and unless these words are accompanied by me, do not send them anywhere she could hear them; also be sure to adorn them with sweet music where I shall be present whenever this is necessary." Having said these words he disappeared, and my sleep was broken.)

But how can Love speak this way? The white-robed figure, reminiscent of St. Mark's angelic guard at the tomb of Christ, who at the beginning had been concerned only with trancendental values, is now interested in giving practical advice—encouraging the lover, in fact, to seek again the kind of happiness that can only fail, to concern himself again with *simulacra?* And the elegant speaker of sententious, epigrammatic Latin engages in this long-winded chatter? It is clear that with the introduction of this note of familiarity the atmosphere of deep seriousness, of awesome majesty that surrounded the figure of Love at the beginning has entirely disappeared.

It is, of course, the Lesser Aspect that gives this worldly advice, so easy (alas) for the young lover to understand: in the lover's mind the god has turned into the *Amore* of Chapter IX, who is on a plane no higher than that of the lover himself. The last words that we hear the Greater Aspect speak are the peremptory "Non dimandare più che utile ti sia"—which, however, being in Italian, prepare for the shift to the Lesser Aspect, serving as a hinge on which the two parts of the vision turn. That we have to do now with the *Amore* of Chapter IX is shown, not only by the tone of Love's words and the nature of his advice, but also by the fact that in his explanation of Beatrice's decision, when speaking of the lady chosen as the second screen, he calls her ". . . la donna la quale *io ti nominai nel cammino de li sospiri* . . . ," thereby identifying himself with the shabby, dejected figure of the pilgrim-Love. And if it is clear from these words that the one who abets the lover in his superficial program of wooing must be the same as the figure in Chapter IX, it should be just as clear that he cannot possibly be the one who appeared on stage saying, "Fili mi, tempus est. . . ." There has been a shift of identity. And since such a vision as this is comparable to a dream, in which one figure may easily turn into another, this shift in the lover's mind needs no psychological justification.

Now that we have recognized the possibility of a shift from the one to the other aspect of Love when this figure appears on stage to speak to the lover, it is only natural to wonder if this will be realized in the next appearance of Love to be considered—that is, the first of the four appearances of Love in the *Vita nuova*. As the lover is sleeping sweetly, after having received Beatrice's first greeting, a marvelous vision comes to him in which he sees first a flame-colored cloud, then a figure in the cloud, whose aspect is frightening to look upon, yet expresses the deepest happiness. He speaks to the lover at length, though only a few of his words such as "Ego dominus tuus" are understandable to him. As he speaks, the lover sees that this awesome figure is holding in his arms a sleeping female figure, naked except for a crimson cloth in which she is loosely wrapped.[8] Slowly the lover recognizes her as his lady; he also notes that the lordly man (who we know must be Love) holding the lady has in his hand a burning object; and he hears the words "Vide cor tuum." After some time has passed Love awakens the lady and cunningly forces her to eat of the burning object. This she does, reluctantly. After another passage of time Love's joy turns to bitterest grief and weeping he folds his arms about the lady and ascends with her toward Heaven. The lover's anguish at their departure breaks his sleep.

This figure who comes during the first of the last nine hours of the night, in the midst of a cloud the color of flame (suggesting the burning bush in which God appeared to Moses), who speaks in Latin and announces his lordship over the lover, and whose aspect is both radiant and terrifying is, obviously, the Greater Aspect of Love. At the end he ascends to Heaven; thus, the figure who appears with Beatrice and who departs with her must represent the same Aspect. And it must also be this divine being who, in the middle of the episode, says to the lover "Vide cor tuum." But I believe that in the lines following these words, in the interval of time that elapsed between Love's last words and the lady's awakening, there has been a shift from the Greater to the Lesser Aspect. "Vide cor tuum" is followed by *E quando elli era stato alquanto, pareami che disvegliasse questa che dormia. . . .* After the lady is made to eat the heart reluctantly, there is another pause in the action before the figure of Love, now weeping, will disappear: *Appresso ciò poco dimorava che la sua letizia si convertìa in amarissimo pianto*—a pause allowing for a second shift of Aspect, back to the first again. That the author has taken pains twice to indicate a lapse of time must be significant; and that his intention has been to set off this central action, to differentiate it from what precedes and what follows, is highly likely. And these two breaks could serve not only as dividers but to allow time for something to happen during the intervals in which nothing seems to happen.

Beatrice asleep in Love's arms is Beatrice dead, already in glory, pure spirit. When she is awakened she becomes a woman of flesh and blood, and her nakedness takes on warmth in the imagination. Perfect Love could not desire such a return to the carnal. Perfect Love could not try to force, to seduce the Belovèd into an act against her nature, as the figure of Love does here:

> E quando elli era stato alquanto, pareami che disvegliasse questa che dormia; e tanto si sforzava per suo ingegno, che le facea mangiare questa cosa che in mano li ardea, la quale ella mangiava dubitosamente.

> (And after some time had passed, he seemed to awaken the one who slept, and he forced her cunningly to eat of that burning object in his hand; she ate of it timidly.)

When the figure of Perfect Love returns once more to the lover's imagination, the figure can only weep. He weeps because the lover's heart which he had declared to be in his possession ("Vide cor tuum") has been given over to the Lesser Love, which would make carnal the spiritual and, because of its covetousness, could envisage arousing covetousness in the miraculous Beatrice. It is difficult to understand the attitude of those critics who find sublimity in Love's gruesome act of forcing the lady to eat the lover's heart.

Now that the four visions have been discussed in the order: 4–3–2–1 (for reasons which should have become rather clear), let us sum up the sequence again in its original order.[9] The figure of love capable of representing either the Greater or the Lesser Aspect, appears for the first time in Chapter III at its most dynamic and paradoxical: shifting from the Greater to the Lesser, back to the Greater Aspect again. The sonnet that the lover writes describing the vision with a minimum of detail, he sends to his literary friends challenging them to discover its significance. And in the chapter immediately following we are told that for some time after his vision his digestive system was so upset that his friends were concerned about his haggard appearance. The literary maneuver may be a sign that the meaning of the vision was not clear to the poet-protagonist (not that such a sign is necessary), and the bad health which followed suggests that the memories of it must have tortured him.

In Chapter IX Love appears in abject form as the symbol of the protagonist-lover's superficial dalliance with the screen-ladies. There are two details in the description of this figure which were passed over in the first discussion of Chapter IX and which are very important for establishing a link with the preceding vision. First, the pilgrim-Love is carrying the lover's heart in his hand, taking it, he says to the new screen-lady. Now, in Chapter III it is clearly the Greater Love that comes on stage with the young lover's heart in his possession; but I suggested that in the central episode of this vision the lover had given it over to the Lesser Love—who, in Chapter IX, still has it. The second link with the vision of Chapter III is of a different sort: in the second quatrain of the sonnet ("Cavalcando l'altrier . . .")[10] following the prose narrative, the figure of Love, who will advise the lover about the second screen-lady, is described as having suffered a change: "Ne la sembianza mi parea meschino,/ come avesse perduto segnoria." The "segnoria" that has been lost is the majesty of the radiant figure who presented himself to the lover saying, "Ego dominus tuus," in his first appearance. In the chapter that follows, the lover earnestly puts into practice the god's advice: the first of two times he will carry out the suggestion of the Lesser Love.

Nine chapters after his first appearance the Greater Love returns to the stage of the *Vita nuova*, again waking the lover, again speaking Latin. This time there is no vague reference to "molte cose" spoken by Love which the lover did not understand. Apparently he said to him only two things in Latin, then turned to Italian to rebuke him sharply. The peremptory words, with the sudden shift from Latin to Italian, serve a purpose ultimately similar to the "lapses of time" indicated in Chapter III, only that whereas the latter allow for something unexpected to happen, for something to emerge out of the interval of time, the rebuke in Italian comes as a sharp announcement of change already on its way.

The obvious connection between the Lesser Love who will come to dominate the stage in Chapter XII, and the pilgrim-Love of Chapter IX has already been pointed out—a connection insisted on by Love himself (". . . la donna la quale *io ti nominai* nel cammino de li sospiri"). I would add that there is also a connection between this figure in Chapter XII, now giving elaborate instructions as to the means of winning back Beatrice's favor, and the one in Chapter III who, in the central episode, was intent on seducing Madonna: that Love who forced the lady with all his art to eat the lover's burning heart.[11] And it is the influence of the Lesser Aspect that continues beyond the vision described: in the *ballata*, concluding the chapter, which the lover dutifully wrote at this figure's command. And it is surely in order that the influence of the Lesser Love should prolong itself beyond the vision that the poem closing the chapter represents this fulfillment of Love's worldly advice rather than sets forth a "recapitulative" version of the vision—the only vision of Love's appearance not described in verse, as was pointed out but not explained in the first part of this essay.

But it becomes clear in the following chapter that the first part of the vision, in which the Greater Love had spoken words the lover did not understand, had also made a strong impression on him. For this chapter is devoted to a "battle of the thoughts" about the nature of love:

Appresso di questa soprascritta visione, avendo già dette le parole che Amore m'avea imposte a dire, mi cominciaro molti e diversi pensamenti a combattere e a tentare, ciascuno quasi indefensibilemente; tra li quali pensamenti quattro mi parea che ingombrassero più lo riposo de la vita. L'uno de li quali era questo: buona è la signoria d'Amore, però che trae lo intendimento del suo fedele da tutte le vili cose. L'altro

*era questo: non buona è la signoria d'Amore, però che quanto
lo suo fedele più fede li porta, tanto più gravi e dolorosi
punti li conviene passare. L'altro era questo: lo nome
d'Amore è sì dolce a udire, che impossibile mi pare che la
sua propria operazione sia ne le più cose altro che dolce, con
ciò sia cosa che li nomi seguitino le nominate cose, sì come
è scritto:* Nomina sunt consequentia rerum. *Lo quarto era
questo: la donna per cui Amore ti stringe così, non è come
l'altre donne, che leggeramente si muova del suo cuore. E
ciascuno mi combattea tanto che mi facea stare quasi come
colui che non sa per qual via pigli lo suo cammino, e che
vuole andare e non sa onde se ne vada; e se io pensava di
volere cercare una comune via di costoro, cioè là ove tutti
s'accordassero, questa era via molto inimica verso me, cioè
di chiamare e di mettermi ne le braccia de la Pietà. E in
questo stato dimorando, mi giunse volontade di scriverne
parole rimate; e dissine allora questo sonetto, lo quale comincia:* Tutti li miei penser.

(After this last vision, when I had already written what Love
commanded me to write, many and diverse thoughts began
to assail and try me, against which I was defenseless; among
these thoughts were four that seemed to disturb most my
peace of mind. The first was this: the lordship of Love is
good since he keeps the mind of his faithful servant away
from all evil things. The next was this: the lordship of Love
is not good because the more fidelity his faithful one shows
him, the heavier and more painful are the moments he must
live through. Another was this: the name of Love is so sweet
to hear that it seems impossible to me that the effect itself
should be in most things other than sweet, since, as has often
been said, names are the consequences of the things they
name: *Nomina sunt consequentia rerum.* The fourth was
this: the lady through whom Love makes you suffer so is
not like other ladies, whose heart can be easily moved to
change its attitude. And each one of these thoughts attacked
me so forcefully that it made me feel like one who does not
know what direction to take, who wants to start and does
not know which way to go. And as for the idea of trying
to find a common road for all of them, that is, one where

all might come together, this was completely alien to me: namely, appealing to Pity and throwing myself into her arms. While I was in this mood, the desire to write some poetry about it came to me, and so I wrote this sonnet which begins: *All my thoughts*.)

The problem he is struggling with is basically the eternal theme of the paradoxical nature of love. Still, it can be no coincidence that the only time he concerns himself with this *topos* is after the vision which contains conflicting aspects of Love. Perhaps the first of the four thoughts that comes to him, which stresses moral values, represents an attempt to think in terms of the Greater Aspect. The second thought, obviously, can apply only to the Lesser Aspect. The third merely describes the familiar oxymoric nature of love, with a touch of scholastic coloring. Whether the last thought is simply the conventional regret that the lady is unyielding, or whether it contains the recognition of the uniqueness of his lady Beatrice, is not too clear. But at least it is undeniable that the lover has been struggling with the problem of the nature of love after a second vision opposing Love's two natures.

In my treatment of the vision in Chapter XXIV, a number of fine details were left undiscussed, since I was faced with the problem of establishing for the first time the identity of the figure of Love. To understand the full significance of this vision the reader should examine carefully the opening lines of the chapter, that set the stage for Love's appearance:

Appresso questa vana imaginazione, avvenne uno die che, sedendo io pensoso in alcuna parte, ed io mi sentio cominciare un tremuoto nel cuore, così come se io fosse stato presente a questa donna. Allora dico che mi giunse una imaginazione d'Amore; che mi parve vederlo venire da quella parte ove la mia donna stava, e pareami che lietamente mi dicesse nel cor mio: "Pensa di benedicere lo dì che io ti presi, però che tu lo dei fare." E certo me parea avere lo

*cuore sì lieto, che me non parea che fosse lo mio cuore, per
la sua nuova condizione. E poco dopo queste parole che lo
cuore mi disse con la lingua d'Amore, io vidi venire verso
me una gentile donna, la quale era di famosa bieltade, e fue
già molto donna di questo primo mio amico.*

(After this wild dream I happened one day to be sitting in a
certain place deep in thought, when I felt a tremor begin in
my heart, as if I were in the presence of my lady. Then a
vision of Love came to me, and I seemed to see him coming
from that place where my lady dwelt, and he seemed to say
joyously from within my heart: "See that you bless the day
that I took you captive; it is your duty to do so." And it
truly seemed to me that my heart was happy, so happy that
it did not seem to be my heart because of this change.
Shortly after my heart had said these words, speaking with
the tongue of Love, I saw coming toward me a gentlewoman,
noted for her beauty, who had been the much-loved lady of
my best friend.)

The "vana imaginazione" mentioned in the opening line is the
prophetic vision of Beatrice's death. That a connection exists
between that vision, described in terms suggesting the Crucifixion, and this one in which Beatrice is indirectly compared
to Christ, is obvious. In fact, the lover might not have been
capable of having this last vision of Love until after having
experienced the one prophetic of her death; this is surely
suggested by the words of Love himself that describe the
significance of the name of Beatrice's companion, Primavera.
He tells the lover:

*"Quella prima è nominata Primavera solo per questa venuta
d'oggi; ché io mossi lo imponitore del nome a chiamarla
così Primavera, cioè 'prima verrà' lo die che Beatrice si
mostrerà dopo la imaginazione del suo fedele. . . ."*

("The one in front is called Primavera only because of the
way she comes today; for I inspired the giver of her name
to call her Primavera, meaning 'she will come first' (*prima*

verrà) on the day that Beatrice shows herself after the dream of her faithful one. . . .")

Thus Love had planned this vision in advance, a plan which involved his inspiring one of Giovanna's friends to give her the nickname Primavera—intending this vision to take place after the vision of Beatrice's death, after the "vana imaginazione."

We are also told, in the opening sentence of the chapter, that the lover's heart began to tremble just before the appearance of Love; the fact that this tremor was of the sort he was accustomed to have when in the presence of his lady, prepares the way for the assimilation of Beatrice to Love at the conclusion of the vision. But this assimilation had already been suggested by degrees: the figure who appears in Chapter III, enveloped in a flame-colored cloud, will reappear in Chapter XII clothed in a garment of purest white; thus, Beatrice's two colors, red and white, belong to the god of Love.

Finally, there is the remarkable fusion between the god and the lover-protagonist, a fusion that takes place almost immediately: he sees Love only briefly, coming from a certain direction; when he hears him speak, the words of Love come from the lover's heart. In the three visions preceding that of Chapter XXIV the Lesser Aspect of Love had been represented: Chapter IX was exclusively concerned with this Aspect, while Chapters III and XII contained a shift from the Greater to the Lesser. And in all three cases this Aspect had been taken as being identical with the lover's feelings at the moment, so far below the level of the Greater Aspect that he could not understand him in the two cases when this being spoke to him. Here, in Chapter XXIV, as we have seen, there is no shift from the Greater to the Lesser; at the same time, however, there is no contrast between the mood of the god and that of the lover-at-the-moment. He has understood him completely, for now the god is speaking from within the lover's heart. For the first time the lover's feelings of the moment have been raised to the height of the Greater Aspect.[12]

And after this high point reached in Chapter XXIV we shall not see the figure of Love again. But surely the young lover does. In that final vision which he withholds from us, which inspired him to stop writing about his love for Beatrice until he could do so more worthily, he must have seen Beatrice in glory; already in Chapter XLI he had caught a glimpse of

> . . . *una donna, che receve onore*
> *e luce sì, che per lo suo splendore*
> *lo peregrino spirito la mira.*

> (. . . a lady held in reverence,
> splendid in light, and through her radiance
> the pilgrim spirit looks upon her being.)

And if he sees, at the end, the celestial radiance of Beatrice, how could the figure of Love be absent from his imagination— Love who had proclaimed the Christlike nature of Beatrice and her likeness to himself. And this time, too, the lover must have been raised to the level of the Greater Aspect, never again to sink below it.

*　　*　　*

In the preceding chapter of this essay, when Dante's predilection for "mathematical thinking" was discussed, the importance of the number 9 was mentioned, its significance being due to the fact that it is the square of 3 which itself represents the Trinity. Because of the symbolic value of this number and the fact that in Chapter XXIX it is made to explain the miracle of Beatrice, one might have expected to find a pattern of "three's" in the structure of the *Vita nuova*. But apart from the three "spiriti" of the lover, mentioned only once, and the three *canzoni*, devoted to Beatrice at different stages of her apotheosis (Beatrice desired by Heaven, Beatrice ascending to Heaven, Beatrice in Heaven), there is no suggestion of such patterning.[13] This is likely to be particularly surprising to the reader of the *Vita nuova* who comes to it from the *Divine Comedy*, where he is invited so often to think in terms of "three" (and always in *terza rima*). What we do find in the *Vita nuova* is an overwhelming emphasis on "two."

Two ladies ask the lover for some of his poetry, toward the close of the book, two ladies at the beginning accompany the eighteen-year-old Beatrice on her first important promenade into the story. In Chapter IX a pilgrim appears, and in Chapter XL, a group of pilgrims. The lover chooses two screen-ladies. There are two persons who are brought on stage to address the lover: one to answer the lover's question (the friend who takes him to the wedding feast in Chapter XIV), the other to question him (the lady in Chapter XVIII who pins him down about his love)—and in both these chapters the young lover is mocked.

There are two roles for the author of the *Vita nuova:* scribe and glossator, and there are two Beatrice's: Beatrice alive and Beatrice dead. Twice we are reminded of the two Beatrice's when, at a time she is still living in the story, she is referred to in terms that could apply only to Beatrice dead.[14] Two colors are mentioned: red and white. Twice in the visions the color red is associated with her; twice the color white is connected with her: once in the story, once in a vision. There are only two concrete objects in the *Vita nuova:* a bed and some "panels" (*certe tavolette*) on which the lover is drawing the figures of angels. Twice in the story a stream of water flows alongside the lover's path.

There are two languages in the *Vita nuova*. The three "spiriti" speak in Latin as does the god of Love, and Latin is used in quotations from the Bible. There are exactly two quotations from the Bible in the narrative proper, and there are two visions in which Love speaks in Latin. And whether the god of Love is speaking in Italian or Latin, he always makes two speeches to the lover. There are, of course, two styles in the *Vita nuova:* that of prose and that of poetry. There are two positions for the *divisioni:* up to Chapter XXXI the *divisione* follows the poem; from this point on it precedes. And there are exactly two periphrases for the city of Florence.

Two chapters of the forty-two are composed of essays; two chapters contain a didactic interpolation; two chapters contain not one but two poems. Two chapters, and only two, contain no reference to Beatrice. There are two chapters in which the protagonist's liver ("lo spirito naturale") is mentioned and two chapters containing visions in which his heart, as an object, is mentioned. In one chapter there is a poem with two beginnings, in another a *canzone* composed of only two stanzas. In two of the visions Love shifts from the greater to the Lesser Aspect.

One must wonder at the meaning, if any, of this apparently completely heterogeneous list. It is surely not to be explained by any Christian symbolic value adhering to the number two; still, within the *Vita nuova*, this number has its own significance: it must reflect the twofold nature of the God of Love. Does this mean that each of the pairs represents somehow the two Aspects? This is obviously true in one case: the pair mentioned last on our list involves the two shifts from the Greater to the Lesser Aspect. It is also true of the poem with two beginnings in Chapter XXXIV. The lover began the sonnet with a calm and reverent allusion to Beatrice's soul in Heaven:

> *Era venuta ne la mente mia*
> *la gentil donna che per suo valore*
> *fu posta da l'altissimo signore*
> *nel ciel de l'umiltate, ov'è Maria.*

> (Into my mind had come the gracious image
> of the lady who, rewarded for her virtue,

was called by His most lofty Majesty
to the calm realm of Heaven where Mary reigns.)

Then he shifts to a new theme, suggesting his own grief over
Beatrice's death, and goes so far as to predicate Love's grief:

> *Era venuta ne la mente mia*
> *quella donna gentil cui piange Amore,*
> *entro 'n quel punto che lo suo valore*
> *vi trasse a riguardar quel ch'eo facia.*

> (Into my mind had come the gracious image
> of the lady for whom Love still sheds his tears,
> just when you were attracted by her virtue
> to come and see what I was doing there.)

There is no question but that here we have a movement from
the Greater to the Lesser Aspect, reminding the reader of the
dramatic exchange of roles on the part of Love himself in
Chapters III and XII. Again, of the two hearts mentioned in
Chapters III and IX, the first was in the possession of the
Greater Love, the second was carried by the Lesser Love. Also,
though this may verge on the pedantic, the double role of
the author (narrator, glossator) may be seen as reflecting the
same duality: the narrator who records, mainly, the imperfect
love of the protagonist, and the glossator who has come to
understand what love for Beatrice must be. The most striking
pair of oppositions is that of the two quotations from the
Bible, both from *Lamentations*. In Chapter VII the protagonist
writes a poem of sham grief beginning with the words, "O voi
che per la via d'Amor passate," telling us in the *divisione* that it
is a modification of Jeremiah's words: "O vos omnes qui transitis per viam. . .". Chapter XXVIII, announcing the death
and ascent into glory of Beatrice, begins with the words of the
same prophet: "Quomodo sedet sola civitas plena populo!"

Again, it may be that one member of the pair will be suggestive of the Lesser Aspect, while the other will be associated

with the theme of pure praise of the lady—surely an important step in the direction of the Greater Aspect. Of the two characters whom we hear address the lover, the first one is the friend who took him to that fateful wedding feast in Chapter XIV where his lovesick appearance provokes the derision of the ladies; the second one is the lady in Chapter XVIII whose question to the lover leads to his announcement of the program of praise he pretends to have adopted. As for the two streams which, I suggest, may represent sources of inspiration, it is the Lesser Love who in Chapter IX gazes into the stream, then to offer the lover advice about a second screen-lady; in Chapter XIX it is after the lover looks into the stream that there come to him the words "Donne ch'avete intelletto d'amore."

These are the only pairs in which the relationship between the two members concerns the development of the protagonist. There are a number, however, in which this relationship is meaningful, and in some cases, is of real importance for the story. Mainly, this significance, slight or great, is obvious. Surely the pilgrims of Chapter XL must remind the reader of the pilgrim figure in Chapter IX—whose trivial concerns offer a contrast to those of the pilgrims on their way to Rome, indifferent to things of this world, their thoughts centered on their holy goal. Of greater importance is the duality of "Beatrice alive—Beatrice dead" (reminding the reader of the parallels offered by the life of Saint Alexis and the *Song of Roland*, in both of which the protagonist's death confers upon him a new significance and makes of him a source of new inspiration), the importance of this duality being reflected in the two periphrases used for the name of the city of Florence, which is referred to only as the city where Beatrice lived or where she died. And we remember that Beatrice alive is twice described in terms of Beatrice dead. The importance of this duality is also reflected in the shift of position of the *divisioni:* it is only after

Beatrice's death that the *divisione* follows the poem (now the reader sees why the author of the *Vita nuova* chose to postpone this artistic improvement until Chapter XXXI).

As for the two styles in which the *Vita nuova* is written, prose and poetry, the combination of the two represents a new literary genre in Italian literature. That the only two colors should be colors susceptible of symbolic interpretation and attributed to Beatrice needs no explanation. That the reader's attention should be called to only two concrete objects is also understandable, but some analysis is required if we would see the relation between the bed in Chapter XXIII and the panels in XXXIV which the lover uses in drawing forms of angels. It was on this bed that the young lover was lying when in his delirium he witnessed the portents of his lady's death. And it is exactly one year after her death that he is sitting, thinking of her, drawing on these panels; he is surely, on this anniversary, remembering his vision of her death, and perhaps the angels that take form on the "certe tavolette" are those that he saw from his bed of delirium, as they ascended to Heaven.

Still more analysis is required to see the significance of the two ladies at the end of the *Vita nuova* who make a request for some of the lover's poems, or the two at the beginning who are with Beatrice when she first greets the protagonist. Why should two (unknown) ladies join in a request for his poetry? and why was Beatrice not accompanied by a group of ladies or by just one lady? As for the scene in which Beatrice makes her first appearance as a young lady, I suggest that the duality, taken first as a minimal indication of plurality, is intended to suggest that *entourage* of feminine beings without which the figure of the Florentine Beatrice would be unimaginable. And if the duality be interpreted strictly and as subordinated to her own uniqueness, then the two ladies are there so that Beatrice may be associated, visually, with the number 3.

Surely these two ladies are the same as the ones who inspire the poem that closes the *Vita nuova:* the description of the lover's spirit gazing with awe at the radiance of Beatrice in glory. These two ladies, who do not appear but merely send word to the young man they once saw receive Beatrice's first greeting, are now deprived of her company. And he grants their request by choosing two of his poems for them, and exceeds their request by composing a third—it is made clear to the reader that the lover sends two poems plus one; and, in the one, he recreates for them the Beatrice that they and he have lost.

As for the two chapters in which Beatrice is not mentioned, the context supplies the explanation. Chapter XX contains the sonnet "Amore e 'l cor gentil sono una cosa" which treats of love generically, of the "saggia donna" and the effect of her beauty on all men. There is an elegance here in the poet's discreet omission of any reference to his lady (an omission which he will more than make up for in the next chapter). The lack of any reference to her in Chapter XXXIV has a shameful motivation: the lover has been swept into rapturous infidelity at the sight of the "lady at the window." But what is most significant, of course, about the negative count of two here illustrated is the positive fact that every other chapter does contain a reference to Beatrice.

Finally, there are pairs whose existence would appear to be a coincidence. What can possibly be the significance of the fact that Chapters VIII and XXVII contain two sonnets, or that in all four visions in which Love appears, he addresses the lover twice? Why are there two mentions of the lover's liver? Why are there two chapters with essays and two chapters with interpolations? Why does the lover choose two screen-ladies?

It is, of course, possible that only coincidence accounts for this last group of "two's" but it is more likely that Dante went out of his way to impress "duality" upon the reader's consciousness—pure duality without any specific significance to detract from the purity. Perhaps there is underlying here something in common with the symbolism underlying the *terza rima* of the *Divine Comedy*. The three beasts of *Inferno I* invite us to think of the major vices, while the three canticles present Hell, Purgatory and Heaven. But the pattern of three lines that continuously recurs as the heart-beat of the poem has no significance except that of "threeness": the pure symbol of the Trinity. And the purity of duality given by the last group of "two's" may be a clear reflection of the Great Duality which represents the major theme and underlying movement of the *Vita nuova*.[15]

III *Growth*

The dual nature of the god of Love was, of course, only a reflection of the potentialities of the young lover's heart. And the rest of this essay, in fact, will be devoted to a study of his heart: his inner conflicts and spiritual development as a lover. The tendency of the critics is to see this development optimistically, and to fix the turning point of the poet-lover's progress in his inspired decision to write the *canzone* "Donne ch'avete intelletto d'amore."

And indeed, according to the prose narrative, Dante wrote this poem as the result of having found a "new matter" for his poetry, of having adopted a new attitude toward his beloved Beatrice—after she refused him her greeting. He comes to realize that, placing his happiness as he had in the ecstasy inspired by her greeting, he had been embracing a false ideal; from now on he would think only of that which could never fail him: the lady Beatrice's excellence itself. And his love for her would express itself only in words of praise. This stage is reached in Chapter XVIII, thanks to his meeting with a group of ladies, one of whom proves to be the inspiration for his new program. Properly enough, the first of his poems of praise is addressed to "Donne che avete intelletto d'amore."[1]

The story of his love begins in Chapter II: Beatrice makes her first appearance and, by the time the chapter ends, nine years have passed with the protagonist under the domination of love. The action starts to flow again in Chapter III when the young lover receives Beatrice's first greeting and, ecstatic, goes home to sleep and to dream that Love appears to him. Soon after this vision his health becomes impaired (IV); his appearance causes concern to his friends and provokes malicious questioning from others who, he deduces, must be jealous of him. In Chapter V a coincidental meeting of glances inspires in the lover the decision to choose a beautiful lady as a screen for his love of Beatrice, and he begins writing poems to the screen-lady, none of which he includes in his little book. After "several years and several months," the screen-lady leaves Florence (VII) and the lover deliberately decides to write a poem pretending deep grief.[2]

The thread of the love story is lost in Chapter VIII, which the author devotes to describing the death of a young lady, one of Beatrice's companions. In Chapter IX he is in the midst of a journey away from Florence. In his sadness over leaving the place where Beatrice is, he imagines that he sees the figure of Love; the god bids him seek a second screen-lady calling her by name. If in Chapter VI the poet has summed up briefly the time spent in service of his first screen-lady, he uses even fewer words in Chapter X to describe his busy wooing of the second. In fact, before the end of the first sentence we begin to learn of the results of his courtship: ". . . la feci mia difesa tanto, che troppa gente ne ragionava oltre li termini de la cortesia . . ." In this brief account there is the momentum and impact of three different movements: his overzealous efforts to convince the lady and the world of a love he did not feel, the stirring up of public opinion which hastened from criticism to slander, and finally, the single act which brought both movements to a halt on the fatal day that Beatrice refused her greeting.[3] The dynamics of this brief, condensed chapter has no parallel in the *Vita nuova*. And, as if to suggest the shock received by the lover, there is no mention in this chapter of his emotional reaction to Beatrice's rejection.[4]

Nor is his reaction mentioned in the chapter that follows—which goes back in time to describe, in lingering detail and by stages, the blissful effect that his lady's greeting has had on him for years (the period of anticipation, the moment of the greeting, the aftermath of lingering ecstasy). Now we can read of his past exaltation, knowing already that this is something that he will never experience again: Chapter XI is a reminiscent pause between the sudden cruel blow dealt the lover by his lady and the outburst of his anguished feelings which must have immediately followed it, but which we learn about only in Chapter XII.[5] The chapter begins with his tears (it is the first time he weeps because of Beatrice). He goes to a solitary place and, after his sobbing has quieted down somewhat, he closes himself in his room to fall asleep like a little boy crying from a spanking. That this is not the tragic grief of a mature person is shown by the concluding simile: "come un pargoletto batuto lagrimando."[6] While the lover sleeps he has his third vision of Love—as a result of which he will send Beatrice a *ballata* imploring her mercy (the first poem he has ever written for her), which will have no effect.

In Chapter XIV is described the scene of his humiliation at the wedding feast, which prompts him to write Beatrice a reproachful sonnet. After this public fiasco the lover is seized by a mood of persistent self-questioning (XV): why seek out Beatrice when the sight of her has such a disastrous effect on him and makes of him such a ludicrous figure? He comes to the realization that whenever he calls to mind her beautiful image, he is overwhelmed by a desire to see her, a desire so strong that it obscures his memory of past experiences. He writes her a sonnet describing again his feelings in her presence, and upbraiding her for the cruelty of her mockery which must kill all pity in others. This sonnet receives the most elaborate *divisioni* so far recorded in the *Vita nuova*.

In Chapter XVI he continues to wrestle with similar thoughts and writes a sonnet about them, again to Beatrice. But then, realizing the futility of such outpourings, the protagonist decides (XVII) to be silent about his own condition, even if this means he will never write to her again. And, in fact, he never does.

It is clear that up until the point when the poet-lover arrives at this decision his love has been entirely self-centered, and mainly puerile and sickly. After the description in Chapter II of Beatrice's beauty, which was praised in panegyrical terms, terms even suggestive of her mystery, she has been presented exclusively, in the following chapters, as the stimulus for his emotions: his ecstasy or his despair. The first feeling reaches its culmination in the rhapsodic description of the threefold effect on him of her greeting; the second, in the very bitter chapters telling of the *gabbo* and its results, which lead to his decision to seek a new theme for his poetry.

The poem, "Donne ch'avete . . . ," which is the result of this decision and of the lover's conversation with the ladies in Chapter XVIII, should be divided, according to its author, into three main parts: I, II–III–IV, V. The *canzone* has a circular movement: I and V are alike in that they both contain apostrophes—the first addressed to the ladies, the last to the *canzone* itself. Moreover, in the first stanza there is briefly created a social *ambiente* of gentility, when the lover promises to talk of Beatrice with the "Donne e donzelle amorose" as his select audience; and in the last stanza there is a return to this *ambi-*

ente, as the poem is instructed to associate, in its journey to the lady, only with courteous folk. Thus, the *canzone* is framed by a social background.

But in stanza II, immediately, without transition, the *ambiente* has changed from the social to the celestial: "Angelo clama in divino intelletto." In the opening line the Divine Intellect suddenly receives the ecstatic exclamation (note the solemnity of the Latinate *clama*) of an angel who has just perceived the splendor of a radiance emanating from Earth, penetrating Heaven, and has recognized the miracle of Beatrice. Then, all of Heaven shouts for this lady. In the admonitory words of Pity there is briefly adumbrated the figure of the wistful lover —which immediately fades as the stern voice is heard, in the last two lines, of one proclaiming to the damned in Hell that he has beheld the hope of the Blessèd:

> *e che dirà ne lo inferno: 'O mal nati,*
> *io vidi la speranze de' beati.'*

> (and who shall say unto the damned in Hell:
> "I have beheld the hope of Heaven's blest.")[7]

The first line of stanza III, offering a gentle transition, is a reminder that, while the figure of Beatrice passes before the people down on earth, these are looking upon one already coveted by Heaven:

> *Madonna è disiata in sommo cielo.*
> *Or voi di sua virtù farvi savere.*
> *Dico, qual vuol gentil donna parere*
> *vada con lei, che quando va per via,*
> *gitta nei cor villani Amore un gelo,*
> *per che onne lor pensero agghiaccia e pere;*
> *e qual soffrisse di starla a vedere*
> *diverria nobil cosa, o si morria.*
> *E quando trova alcun che degno sia*
> *di veder lei, quei prova sua vertute,*

ché li avvien, ciò che li dona, in salute,
e sì l'umilia, ch'ogni offesa oblia.
Ancor l'ha Dio per maggior grazia dato:
che non pò mal finir chi l'ha parlato.

(My lady is desired in highest heaven.
Now let me tell you something of her power.
A lady who aspires to graciousness
should seek her company for, where she goes,
Love drives a killing frost into vile hearts
that freezes and destroys what they are thinking;
should such a one insist on looking at her,
he is changed to something noble or he dies.
And if she finds one worthy to behold her,
that man will feel her power for salvation
when she accords to him her salutation,
which humbles him, till he forgets all wrongs.
God has graced her with an even greater gift:
whoever speaks with her shall speak with Him.)

This is not the first time that Beatrice has been presented as passing through the streets of Florence; but before this it was as if she were observed by only one person, and as if he alone were impressed by her beauty (II) and her greeting (III). Now, Beatrice's movement forward is witnessed by all the people of Florence, each one of whom is affected by her presence. And here the effect is exclusively on the moral plane: regenerative or punitive according to the merits of the one having the experience of seeing her.

Stanza IV opens with Beatrice receiving the encomium, the superlative encomium of Love ("Dice di lei Amor . . ."), who is presented as gazing steadily upon her—then uttering a prophecy of her apotheosis. Unlike the first two stanzas of praise (II and III) which represent units, each in its own setting, this stanza (which offers no "setting" for Love) falls into three parts. The four lines following the testimony of Love are devoted to a description, the only one in the *Vita nuova*, of

Beatrice's carnal beauty, the coloring of her flesh ("color di perle . . .")—it was an elegant move to postpone this allusion to the beauty of Beatrice's body until after having described the beauty of her soul. By an easy transition, by an allusion to her eyes and their effect upon the beholder, Beatrice comes once more to move among the people of Florence. In the last lines it is not her moral effectiveness that is extolled but her capacity for arousing love, as her glance passes through the eyes of him who looks at her, and reaches his heart.[8] But, of course, for Beatrice to awaken love is for her to awaken love of virtue.

Of the five lyrical poems concerned with his love that precede the first *canzone* (XII, XIII, XIV, XV and XVI), all have in common the lover's need for pity. And all but the *ballata*, in which he affirms his loyalty to Beatrice (XII), describe his sad and sickly state. But the *canzone* is devoted entirely to the glorification of Beatrice. If the lover is present at all in this poem it is only as a figure lost in the mass of Beatrice's admirers, and the reader is never made directly aware, at any point, of the drama of the lover's feelings. Truly a new note has been sounded in the *Vita nuova*.

But the note is new also in Italian poetry: nothing quite comparable can be found in any of the love poetry preceding Dante. It is true that Cavalcanti had written three love poems of pure praise, and Guinizelli at least two;[9] moreover, one of these latter ("Io voglio del ver . . .") offers in the tercets a picture of the moral effects on others of the lady's perfection. In fact, the last lines of this sonnet evoke the same situation as that of the central stanza of Dante's first *canzone:* Guinizelli, too, presents the lady as she passes before others:

> *Passa per via adorna, e sì gentile*
> *ch'abassa orgoglio a cui dona salute,*
> *e fa 'l de nostra fé se non la crede;*

> e nolle pò apressare om che sia vile;
> ancor ve dirò c'ha maggior vertute:
> null' om pò mal pensar fin che la vede.

(With decorum and such grace she passes by,
   and her gift of salutation makes pride bow,
   converting non-believers to our faith;
   no evil man can come within her bounds;
   there is more to tell; even greater powers has she:
   no man can have a base thought in her presence.)

But one detail at least is lacking that was found in Dante's poem, in which Beatrice's efficacy is presented as not only regenerative but punitive: "E qual soffrisse di starla a vedere/ diverria nobil cosa, *o si morria*." This suggests, somehow, the Beatrice of *Purgatory* XXX, come to judge her lover.

And surely there is nothing in earlier literature to compare with the second stanza: the scene in Heaven when the radiance emanating from Beatrice is perceived, and the miracle of her nature recognized by all the *coelestes*—so different from the heavenly scene of recantation that closes Guinizelli's *canzone* which Dante admired so much: "Al cor gentil rempaira sempre amore." Finally, in stanza IV is proclaimed Love's recognition of the Divine plan for Beatrice: ". . . e fra se stesso giura/che Dio ne 'ntenda di far cosa nuova." It was of course a *topos* in medieval love poetry to claim that the lady was created directly by God, from the beginning unique and miraculous, but the "cosa nuova" intended by God in these lines is something still in store for Beatrice. She will become more.

In Chapter XXI Dante writes again in praise of his lady— more briefly, more simply, limiting himself to the sonnet form: "Ne li occhi porta la mia donna Amore." In fact, this sonnet is a reworking of the central stanza (also of fourteen lines) of the first *canzone:* again Beatrice is seen passing before the people who gaze upon her with awe. This is also the theme of the

next two poems of praise, both found in Chapter XXVI. The
first is Dante's most famous sonnet, and one of the most famous
in world literature:

> *Tanto gentile e tanto onesta pare*
> *la donna mia quand'ella altrui saluta,*
> *ch'ogne lingua deven tremando muta,*
> *e li occhi no l'ardiscon di guardare.*
> *Ella si va, sentendosi laudare,*
> *benignamente d'umiltà vestuta;*
> *e par che sia una cosa venuta*
> *dal cielo in terra a miracol mostrare.*
>
> *Mostrasi sì piacente a chi la mira,*
> *che dà per li occhi una dolcezza al core,*
> *che 'ntender no la può chi no la prova:*
> *e par che de la sua labbia si mova*
> *un spirito soave pien d'amore,*
> *che va dicendo a l'anima: "Sospira!"*

> (Such sweet decorum and such gentle grace
> attend my lady's greeting as she moves
> that lips can only tremble into silence,
> and eyes dare not attempt to gaze at her.
> Moving, benignly clothed in humility,
> untouched by all the praise along her way,
> she seems to be a creature come from Heaven
> to earth to manifest a miracle.
>
> Miraculously gracious to behold,
> her sweetness reaches, through the eyes, the heart
> (who has not felt this cannot understand),
> and from her lips it seems there moves a gracious
> spirit, so deeply loving that it glides
> into the souls of men, whispering: "Sigh!")

The first quatrain describes a single, crystalized moment
(which we must imagine forever repeated), the moment of
Beatrice's greeting, with its immediate electrical effect upon
the individual so honored; the second quatrain is all fluidity as

the lady, having come from afar, moves ahead in space and time, to the rhythm of *ella si va;* the apparent break with the tercets is effaced by the fusion of *mostrare* and *Mostrasi.* There is a flow of sweetness, that can only be distilled in a "sigh."— In the second sonnet ("Vede perfettamente onne salute") the lady is seen not alone but attended by other ladies who, somehow, seem to partake of her perfection: ". . . ciascuna per lei receve onore."

In Chapter XXVII we are told that the protagonist, after re-reading the last two sonnets, decides to change his theme, his reason being that he had failed to include in them any reference to himself. And so, finding these poems defective ("pare-ami defettivamente avere parlato"), he begins to write a *canzone* about the effect of Beatrice upon him. But in Chapter XVIII he had decided that from then on he would choose material for his poems that would be only in praise of his lady ("propuosi di prendere per matera de lo mio parlare *sempre mai* quello che fosse loda di questa gentilissima"). How can this reversal of position be explained? Perhaps he believed that with the practice gained by writing four poems of selfless adoration he could take up once again a more personal theme without fear of giving way to self-infatuation; that he could describe the effects of his lady's virtues upon him with the same objectivity he had displayed in describing the reactions of others to his lady's beauty. Moreover, he indirectly promises his reader that he will have something new to say about his feelings ("quello che *al presente tempo* adoperava in me"); and indeed, the calm, opening lines of the *canzone* he was never to finish do suggest a new stage in his feelings:

> Sì lungiamente m'ha tenuto Amore
> e costumato a la sua segnoria,
> che sì com'elli m'era forte in pria,
> così mi sta soave ora nel core.

(So long a time has Love kept me a slave
and in his lordship fully seasoned me,
that even though at first I felt him harsh
now tender is his power in my heart.)

At least we are led to expect a poem of happiness and poise. But, in the lines that follow, it becomes evident that the sweetness of which he speaks ("soave . . . nel core") is still a sickly sweetness. The first detail offered is the loss of his strength: he speaks of his fainting soul and of the pallor of his face, and twice the disequilibrium of his *spiriti* is mentioned. But not only does he offer a morbid description of his condition: the picture of the *spiriti* of sight that are dispossessed by Love has been offered three times before (in the prose of Chapter XI, in the prose and in the poem of Chapter XIV). This repetition gives the impression that he is moved by some mechanical force, and this suggestion of the mechanical is strengthened by the penultimate line with its insistence on the inevitability of this destructive process: "Questo m'avvene ovunque ella mi vede. . . ." And with this fourteen-line stanza ends the poem (interrupted by the death of Beatrice) that was to have been a *canzone* because, as the protagonist had confidently declared, the short form of the sonnet would not have sufficed to describe the "new" state of his feelings. There is, perhaps, poetic justice in the fact that his abortive attempt to describe his supposed new happiness should take the form of an abortive poem.

It is theoretically possible that, if conditions had allowed the protagonist to finish his unfinished *canzone*, the total effect would have been quite different from that made by the opening stanza. Perhaps he would have picked up the note of the last line referring to his lady's "humility" (". . . e sì è cosa umil, che nol si crede") in order, finally, to subordinate his own emotional experience to her excellence. But this is not very likely, in the light of the words with which he describes his own judgment of the two preceding sonnets: "seeing . . . that

I had not mentioned anything about the effect she had on me at the present time, I realized *that I had spoken insufficiently* ('defettivamente')." Not only does he decide to write a poem about himself: he reads over two poems in praise of his lady, including the exquisite sonnet "Tanto gentile e tanto onesta pare," and judges them to be defective on the grounds that they contain no mention of himself! And to remedy the situation he decides that, if he would describe his condition adequately, he should write not a sonnet but a poem as lengthy as his first poem of praise, "Donne ch'avete intelletto d'amore." He was able to allow for the overshadowing of his sonnets of praise by a monument to his own feelings. And, in judging defective the sonnets of Chapter XXVI, it is almost as if he were ready to cancel out the last two poems of praise, thus reducing the total achievement of his new program to two poems (the first *canzone* and the sonnet in Chapter XXI). For our protagonist will never write another poem of praise (that is, one devoted solely to this theme).

The critics, as we know, have considered the protagonist's decision to limit his love poems to praise of the lady as the turning point of the action of the *Vita nuova*, the turning point of his spiritual development as a lover. According to some (e.g. Singleton) the lover goes beyond the stage reached in the first *canzone;* according to others (e.g. De Robertis) there is no higher stage than this reached in the course of the *Vita nuova*. I know of no critic who speaks of the breakdown of his program of praise. But there was a breakdown!

It may well be that the unfinished *canzone* which Dante places immediately after the last poem of praise was actually among the earliest poems of his youthful period. But this would not diminish in the least our right to interpret these lines according to their position in the text. For, whenever it was written and whatever may have been its inspiration, the only fact of importance for the reader of the *Vita nuova*, as I stated in the Preface, is that its author has chosen to place it where he did.[10]

After Chapter XXVIII, in which Beatrice's death is announced, it would be impossible to find poems of praise in the conventional sense, but we might have expected that the shock of her death would have inspired in the lover a new kind of praise concerned only with her heavenly attributes (a suggestion of this was already present in the first *canzone*).[11] But instead of a rekindling of his inspiration, there is a calamitous collapse into his early mood of emotional self-indulgence. The four poems that open the period of his life after Beatrice's death are characterized by the most arrant self-pity: there are five references to sighs, thirteen to tears, and twenty-four to anguish, and there are numerous similar references in the prose that precedes them. The time has come to scrutinize more carefully the poetry of praise contained in the *Vita nuova*, and also to examine, for the first time in detail, the circumstances responsible for the protagonist's adoption of his new program.

As for the events leading up to the adoption of this new program of praise, it is in Chapter XVII, as we know, that the lover decides to abandon the theme of morbid self-analysis. But he also announces, anticipating what he will tell us in the following chapter, that he has found the new theme; and the account of his finding it, he promises, will be pleasant to listen to.

The narrative of Chapter XVIII opens with a background of ladies gathered together enjoying each other's company (with "dilettandosi l'una ne la compagnia de l'altra" we are reminded of the many social scenes in the *Decameron*). These are ladies who happen to be well aware of the protagonist's love and of its disastrous effects on him; as he happens to pass by, one of them hails him. The background of ladies forms a tryptic: some laughing together, some watching him, and some talking together. It is one of these who abruptly asks the lover a question: "To what end do you love this lady of yours, if you cannot resist the sight of her?" She insists on an answer (since the goal of such a love must be strange indeed). With this, the three groups of ladies become one, as all wait for the answer. He replies: "Ladies, the end and aim of my love formerly lay in the greeting of this lady, to whom you are perhaps referring, and in this greeting dwelt the bliss which was the end of all my desires. But since it pleased her to deny it to me, my lord, Love, through his grace, has placed all my bliss in something that cannot fail me." The first response to his sanctimonious remark is a flow of words and sighs from the ladies, which reminds him of the fall of rain mingled with beautiful flakes of snow (and inspires the only complete simile in the *Vita nuova;* see note 6). But one of the ladies, the one who had first hailed him, is not impressed by his verbosity nor is she put off by his evasiveness. She asks him point-blank in what his bliss now consists. He answers, as briefly: "In those words that praise my lady." She retorts: "If you are telling us the truth, then those words you wrote her about your feelings must have been composed with other intentions." And as he leaves the group, he is ashamed and filled with astonishment that he had written as he had.[12] It is then that for the first time he decides to choose praise of his lady as his theme—after hearing himself announce that as his program, forced into this announcement by the insistent prodding of the lady. So, this lady whose only purpose has been to taunt him becomes, in spite of herself, the Muse of his new poetry, a Muse, to be sure, quite different from the usual one, who guides the poetic flight of the poet already possessed of his theme. Here his Muse forces him to find a theme.[13]

But he will not start writing immediately, lacking the boldness to undertake a theme too lofty for his talents, and the chapter ends with his conflicting emotions, his desire to compose and his hesitancy to begin the task. He has still not begun when the next chapter opens. Thinking first in terms of the correct poetic procedure, he decides that his unborn poem can only be addressed to refined ladies. This decided upon, his tongue, he tells us, suddenly moved as if of its own accord and spoke the words "Donne ch'avete intelletto d'amore." Recognizing that this must be the opening line of his poem, he joyfully stored it away in his memory and, after some days of reflection, began to write.

Most critics of the *Vita nuova* speak of the spontaneity of the composition of Dante's magnificent first *canzone*, characteristic of the so-called *dolce stil novo*.[14] But, in the first place, it owes much to pure chance: it is the result of a coincidental meeting (the protagonist himself stresses the fact that he was directed to the ladies as if guided *by fortune*), and of being pushed into a verbal corner.[15] It is also the result of a struggle, the struggle to make good the words forced out of him by an acidulous young lady (one cannot fail to note the untranscendental nature of his Muse). And when his tongue is finally inspired to speak, it speaks in terms only of the audience he has chosen: "Donne ch'avete intelletto d'amore." (In a somewhat similar way he chose the audience for whom he would write his first sonnet, this time an audience composed of fellow-poets.) It is only later, after much reflection, that the real substance of his poem came to him. Given the reluctant nature of his inspiration, it is not surprising that he found this inspiration difficult to sustain for long.

It was said earlier that in the first *canzone* a new note had been sounded, not only in the poetry of the *Vita nuova* but in Italian poetry. But in the three poems of praise that follow, the "new note" is muted: the sternness of Beatrice's demeanor in the middle stanza of the first *canzone*, that seemed to point ahead to the Beatrice of *Purgatory*, has dissolved.[16] Not only do the sonnets offer a more sentimentalized version of the central stanza of the first *canzone*, there is also suggested, in spite of their high poetic quality, taken singly, a certain staleness of imagination. The poet-lover cannot conceive a new situation in which to present Beatrice: three more times he must show her passing before the people, and the purifying effect of her beauty, of her glance.[17]

And what he is repeating, of course, is a concept that he has borrowed from Guinizelli ("Io voglio del ver la mia donna laudare"), who himself, to the best of my knowledge, had borrowed it from no one. At least I know of no love poem in Italian literature before Guinizelli, or in Provençal love poetry, where we find such a blend of sensuous and spiritual beauty in the portrait of a lady, together with an account of the galvanizing effect of her qualities—and this against the delicately suggested background of the society in which the lady lives and which she transforms.[18] Guinizelli (see note 8) concentrated his invention in the tercets of his sonnet; the quatrains are very different. Metaphor is piled on metaphor as the lady is compared to what she is not: from the sweet-smelling rose and lily to the radiant morning star to the bright colors of nature and of art—all suggesting sensuous beauty. Then, after a transitional line with an intimation of the spiritual (line 8), appears the lady herself, the purity of her beauty in the tercets enhanced by the sensuous background of the quatrains. So, Guinizelli invented the theme "the lady passes," presented it as the climax of a sonnet, and never returned to it again. Dante borrowed it, magnified it to the full length of a sonnet, and used it four times to praise his lady. In one case, it is true (the central stanza of the first *canzone*), his adaptation had a power and a sublimity beyond that of its model, but in this one case we have not the climax of an upward movement but a brilliant beginning which is itself the end: there was no further development from this *canzone* in the *Vita nuova*. But how could there be one in this little book? That was to be for another, greater book.

In fact, the first *canzone* is immediately followed by a poem whose theme bears no direct relationship to the main action of the story. It is a generic treatment of the origin of love in the human heart: "Amore e 'l cor gentil sono una cosa." In the first quatrain the identity of love and the gentle heart is proclaimed and insisted upon; the second speaks of their common origin (both created by Nature in an amorous mood) and of the function served by the heart to provide a home in which love may sleep. The tercets describe the three stages preparatory to the awakening of love in the man's heart, the last line attributing the same process to feminine psychology. This line ("E simil face in donna omo valente.") is sheer bathos. And the sonnet as a whole, completely lacking in lyrical inspiration, is weakly imitative: the quatrains are clearly reminiscent of Guinizelli; the tercets could be from any poet from Giacomo da Lentino on—except, perhaps, for the final line.

The lover writes this sonnet, according to the prose explanation that precedes, because a friend, having read "Donne ch'avete intelletto d'amore" (which by this time had become well-known), asked him for his definition of love. And the protagonist decided that, after having treated the theme of Beatrice's excellence, it would be fitting to treat of love in general. We must wonder how anybody who truly appreciated the originality and power of this, one of the greatest *canzoni* in Italian literature, could suggest that its author return to the stale practice of offering a definition of love. But it is even more surprising that the author of "Donne ch'avete intelletto d'amore" should be interested in fulfilling his friend's request. If he believed that he could revitalize this conventional theme, as Guinizelli had done so magnificently in his famous *canzone* ("Al cor gentil . . ."), the reader of the *Vita nuova* might understand his decision, but in the sonnet which the protagonist wrote, supposedly following his friend's suggestion, the staleness is unmitigated; the lack of poetic inspiration is obvious.

And it suffers painfully from its immediate juxtaposition with the *canzone*. To this, one cannot object that the poem may well have been one of the young Dante's earliest poems, for it was the older Dante that decided on such a juxtaposition, just as he decided to give the rather witless motivation for its composition that he did. The author of the *Vita nuova* chose to place one of the weakest poems he had ever written where he did to indicate a decline of the protagonist's creative powers after the high point reached in his first *canzone*. Just how long this diminution of his powers may have lasted is not made specific, but it seems clear that the lover of Beatrice wrote nothing during the time his *canzone* was becoming known. And it would also seem that he was forced to accept gratefully a theme proposed by a friend, only indirectly related to his new program of praise, in order to start writing again.

It would seem, too, that the effort expended in producing this sonnet-by-request gives our protagonist a new momentum (for a while), even suggesting the way to return to his chosen theme: having described the power of any virtuous and beautiful woman, he tells us (XXI) he is inspired now to describe the far greater power of his own lady. He writes the graceful sonnet "Ne li occhi porta la mia donna amore" to be followed in Chapter XXVI by the exquisite "Tanto gentile e tanto onesta pare" and the more modest "Vede perfettamente ogni salute."

In carefully comparing these sonnets with the first *canzone* the reader can only feel, as has been said, that there has been a let-down, but, as we have just seen, these sonnets do not follow the *canzone* immediately. They follow the feeble sonnet written after the great falling away from the *canzone*, and as a continuation of this sonnet they represent an increase in poetic creativity. The protagonist was, after all, able to move upward for a second time and maintain himself on a relatively high plateau before he fell to the low level of the unfinished *canzone* (XXVII), in which he returns to the self-pity of the earlier years before embarking on his new program of praise.[19]

Between Chapters XXI and XXVI, containing the three sonnets of praise, come four more poems: two sonnets on the death of Beatrice's father (XXII), the *canzone* describing the lover's prophetic vision of Beatrice's death (XXIII), and the sonnet dealing with his last vision of Love. Since none of these is a love poem the question of "praise" versus "self-pity" cannot arise. At the same time, however, it is true that the first two offered the protagonist an excellent opportunity to express indirectly whatever grief he may still have been feeling because of the loss of his lady's greeting, channeling the main stream of his grief into tributaries, as it were.

In the prose of Chapter XXII we are told that the lover takes up his stand on a street by which most of the ladies who had gone to Beatrice's home to mourn her father's death would be likely to return. We watch three groups of ladies pass and hear them speak. The first group speak of Beatrice's grief, the second of their own (and their words reduce him to tears); the third group turn their attention to the grief-stricken figure of the lover, whom they recognize, covering his face with his hands. They seem to wonder at his tears since he has not been privileged to see Beatrice weep; they also comment on the change he has undergone since they first knew him—we may be reminded of the three groups of ladies in Chapter XVIII. And as, continuing to speak, they leave him behind, he hears the sound of his name mingled with that of Beatrice.

Both of the poems in Chapter XXII are full of tears. In the first, where the lover pretends to address the grieving ladies who have come from the scene of Beatrice's grief, it is her tears and theirs that are described; in the last line only is there a reference to the feelings of the protagonist touched by the ladies' grief:

Io veggio li occhi vostri c'hanno pianto
e veggiovi tornar sì sfigurate,
che 'l cor mi triema di vederne tanto.

(I see your eyes, I see how they have wept,
and how you come retreating all undone;
my heart is touched and shaken at the sight.)

But the reader is made aware of the vicarious pleasure the lover
is experiencing as he dwells at length on the mourners' expressions of grief. In the second sonnet, in which he pretends that
the ladies returning from Beatrice address him, the first two
quatrains are devoted to his own grief:

Se' tu colui c'hai trattato sovente
   di nostra donna, sol parlando a nui?
   Tu risomigli a la voce ben lui,
   ma la figura ne par d'altra gente.
   E perché piangi tu sì coralmente,
   che fai di te pietà venire altrui?
   Vedestù pianger lei, che tu non pui
   punto celar la dolorosa mente?

(Are you the one that often spoke to us
   about our lady, and to us alone?
   Your tone of voice, indeed, resembles his,
   but in your face we find another look.
   Why do you weep so bitterly? Pity
   would melt the heart of anyone who sees you.
   Have you seen her weep, too, and now cannot
   conceal from us the sorrow in your heart?)

It is true that these words are put into the mouths of the ladies;
the poet-lover does not speak in his own voice to describe his
grief. But what he has done instead makes us even more aware
of his self-centeredness: he has offered us a picture of himself
as seen by others, he has made of himself a theatrical figure of
grief—a grief which supposedly has so ravaged his features as
to make him all but unrecognizable. Not only does his sorrow

over Beatrice's father as it is portrayed here strike the reader as excessive: one must also wonder why, in this account of the protagonist's experience as a lover, *two* poems have been inspired by the father's death. One can only conclude that the occasion offered him the excuse to treat a favorite theme without directly expressing his own feelings. (Ultimately the two poems are artistically justified: concerned as they are with the theme "death of a loved one," they serve to anticipate the *canzone* that immediately follows, containing the lover's vision of Beatrice's death.[20])

After learning of his lady's death, which seems to take place between chapters XXVII and XXVIII, somewhere outside of the world of the *Vita nuova*, the protagonist writes three chapters without a poem. In the first he announces with composure the calling to glory of Beatrice, and enumerates the reasons for not discussing this event; in the second he offers a brief treatise on the significance of the number nine and its relationship to Beatrice; in the third he tells us of having written to the "great of the land" about the desolation of Florence after Beatrice's death.

These three chapters following the death of Beatrice constitute the most arid portion of the *Vita nuova*. No reader can fail to notice the chill of this opening part of the final section of Dante's Book of Memory, and the contrast it offers to the poem that has just preceded. Has the shock of Beatrice's death numbed the protagonist's feelings (if not his memory)? Or has he, feeling shame over the self-pitying mood in which he was caught by the news of her death, resolved to banish all thoughts about his own condition? To one who reads carefully the opening lines of Chapter XXX the first suggestion is patently false; the second is closer to the truth.

> *Poi che fue partita da questo secolo, rimase tutta la sopra-*
> *detta cittade quasi vedova dispogliata da ogni dignitade;*
> *onde io,* ancora lagrimando in questa desolata citade . . .

(After she had departed from this world, the aforementioned city was left as if a widow, stripped of all dignity, and I, *still weeping in this barren city.* . . .)

Evidently, ever since the moment that the lover heard about
Beatrice's death he has been weeping, forcing himself, while he
wept, to think beyond his tears; he wrote his Latin letter
"*ancora* lagrimando." Because of this *ancora* we can reread
Chapter XXVIII with more sympathy, and with admiration
for the task which he had stoically imposed upon himself in
what were perhaps his moments of deepest grief.

Up to the "ancora lagrimando" of Chapter XXX the lover
had been able since the death of his lady to completely hide his
tears from us; and after this passing, almost casual, reference to
his anguish he is able to continue the chapter imperturbably
to its pedantic end. But in Chapter XXXI his self-control
breaks down completely. In the tear-drenched narrative of this
chapter, redolent of emotional decay, the poet-lover announces
the inspiration of what will turn out to be his third and last
canzone: since his eyes are too wept-out to relieve his feelings,
he hopes this relief may be obtained by writing a sad poem
about Beatrice and the destructive effects on him of his grief.
And in order that the melancholy effect of his poem might
linger on, unchecked by the usual *divisione*, he decides to get
it out of the way before the poem begins.

The first stanza opens with a reference to his grieving eyes
that wish to weep, continues with an evocation of the ladies
with whom he used to speak of Beatrice alive, and ends with
the announcement that his theme will be the ascension of Beatrice's soul to Heaven. The second stanza, fittingly enough, is
concerned with his lady in glory. The third stanza follows
without a break as if to invite the reader to continue to medi-
tate on the theme of Beatrice in glory. But then come the
harsh lines:

Chi no la piange quando ne ragiona,
core ha di pietra sì malvagio e vile
ch'entrar no i puote spirito benegno.

(Who speaks of her and does not speak in tears
has a vile heart, insensitive as stone
which never can be visited by love.)

And, after more flagellation of the wicked hearts that do not
weep for Beatrice, the stanza ends with the tears and moans
of the pure-hearted who must of necessity weep. From this
suggestion of a potentially universal grief, the poet returns, in
stanza IV, to the theme of his personal anguish, and to this
theme he devotes entirely the last two stanzas, ending with an
appeal to Beatrice for mercy. The last word of the stanza is
merzede, so reminiscent of the lover's earlier attitude.

The first of the three *canzoni* contained an anticipation of
the death of Beatrice: in the second stanza was powerfully described the eagerness of Heaven to call her: excited by the
splendor of her radiance that has penetrated Heaven from
Earth, the angels recognized the miracle of Beatrice. Now,
time has passed and Heaven has its wish: Beatrice has ascended
to where the beam of her radiance had preceded her. Here in
the third *canzone*, the theme of which is announced as the
ascent of Beatrice to Heaven, the poet-lover has the opportunity (in fact, his choice of theme was a direct challenge to
his powers) to offer a climactic treatment of Beatrice in glory,
the realization of Heaven's wish. But the potential sublimity of
the theme he has chosen not only does not inspire him to tran-
scend his personal grief in the two final stanzas: even in the
single stanza devoted to his theme he can only repeat, much
less powerfully, with much less conviction, the theme of the
second stanza of his first *canzone*. Compare with that picture
of Heaven's eagerness to receive Beatrice, the picture offered
in the third *canzone* of the fulfillment of Heaven's wish:

Ita n'è Beatrice in alto cielo,
  nel reame ove li angeli hanno pace,
  e sta con loro, e voi, donne, ha lassate:
  no la ci tolse qualità di gelo
  né di calore, come l'altre face,
  ma solo fue sua gran benignitate;
  ché luce de la sua umilitate
  passò li cieli con tanta vertute,
  che fè maravigliar l'etterno sire,
  sì che dolce disire
  lo giunse di chiamar tanta salute;
  e fella di qua giù a sé venire,
  perché vedea ch'esta vita noiosa
  non era degna di sì gentil cosa.

(Beatrice has gone home to highest Heaven,
  into the peaceful realm where angels live;
  she is with them; she has left you, ladies, here.
  No quality of heat or cold took her
  away from us, as is the fate of others;
  it was her great unselfishness alone.
  For the pure light of her humility
  shone through the heavens with such radiance,
  it even made the Lord Eternal marvel;
  and then a sweet desire
  moved Him to summon up such blessedness;
  and from down here He had her come to Him,
  because He knew this wretched life on earth
  did not deserve to have her gracious presence.)

To state seriously that Beatrice died because of her virtues and
not because of the extremes of the climate of Florence is to
show lack of poetic inspiration. And this statement is followed
by a rather flat summary of the situation so gloriously described in the first *canzone;* the last three lines simply bring
the reader up to date. This poem, because of the opportunity
which was offered by its theme but not exploited, surely ex-
poses the inadequacy of the poet-lover's inspiration.

The poem that follows this *canzone*, "Venite ad intender li sospiri miei," was written, so Dante tells us in the prose, at the request of Beatrice's brother. The poem speaks of the lover's tears, of his sighs calling upon his lady, of his grief that leads to a desire for death. The following poem (representing the first two stanzas of a *canzone*), also written for the brother, begins with the same dreary tone: "Quantunque volte, lasso, mi ri-membra." This continues into the second stanza—which ends, however, on a quite different note:

> *perché 'l piacere de la sua bieltate,*
> *partendo sé da la nostra veduta,*
> *divenne spiral bellezza grande,*
> *che per lo cielo spande*
> *luce d'amor, che li angeli saluta,*
> *e lo intelletto loro alto, sottile*
> *face maravigliar, sì v'è gentile.*

> (This is because the beauty of her grace,
> withdrawing from the sight of men forever,
> became transformed to beauty of the soul,
> diffusing through the heavens
> a light of love that greets the angels there,
>   moving their subtle, lofty intellects
> to marvel at this miracle of grace.)

In the last five lines we have the picture of Beatrice radiant in Heaven that the poet-lover was not able to achieve in the third *canzone*.

Perhaps encouraged by this slight success he begins a sonnet continuing the same theme in the same tone:

> *Era venuta ne la mente mia*
> *la gentil donna che per suo valore*
> *fu posta da l'altissimo signore*
> *nel ciel de l'umilitate, ov'è Maria.*

> (Into my mind had come the gracious image
> of the lady who, rewarded for her virtue,

was called by His most lofty Majesty
to the calm realm of Heaven where Mary reigns.)

But this is the ill-fated sonnet with two beginnings, the second of which cancels out the first:

Secondo cominciamento
Era venuta ne la mente mia
  quella donna gentil cui piange Amore,
  entro 'n quel punto che lo suo valore
  vi trasse a riguardar quel ch'eo facia.
  Amor, che ne la mente la sentia,
  s'era svegliato nel destrutto core,
  e diceva a' sospiri: "Andate fore;"
  per che ciascun dolente si partia.

Piangendo uscivan for de lo mio petto
  con una voce che sovente mena
  le lagrime dogliose a li occhi tristi.
  Ma quei che n'uscian for con maggior pena,
  venian dicendo: "Oi nobile intelletto,
  oggi fa l'anno che nel ciel salisti."

Second beginning
Into my mind had come the gracious image
  of the lady for whom Love still sheds his tears,
  just when you were attracted by her virtue
  to come and see what I was doing there.
  Love, who perceived her presence in my mind,
  and was aroused within my ravaged heart,
  commanded all my sighs: "Go forth from here!"
  And each one started on his grieving way.

Lamenting, they came pouring from my heart,
  together in a single voice (that often
  brings painful tears to my melancholy eyes);
  but those escaping with the greatest pain
  were saying: "This day, O intellect sublime,
  completes a year since you rose heavenward.")

The glimpse of Heaven offered by the first is eclipsed by a picture of Love in tears. And it is clearly not the first beginning but the second which sets the tone for the rest of this sad sonnet, which stresses not only the lover's grief but its destructive effect on his psyche—a sonnet written to commemorate the first anniversary of Beatrice's ascent to Heaven.

This bicipitous confession of failure is followed immediately by the poems describing his infidelity to Beatrice: the next five chapters with their five sonnets will tell of the lover's infatuation with "the lady at the window" and his recovery therefrom. In Chapter XXXV he catches sight of a lady looking down at him from her window, observing his sad attitude with an expression of pity. Though he turns away in order to hide his abject state, he tells himself as he leaves that there must be perfect love in the heart of such a compassionate lady. A sudden glance at a stranger's face, a sudden welling up of tears, results in the immediate conviction that the pity he has seen must be a warrant of the noblest kind of love! At least, however, he confesses for the first time to self-pity as a weakness from which all men may suffer: ". . . quando li miseri veggiono di loro compassione altrui, più tosto si muovono a lagrimare, *quasi come di se stessi avendo pietade . . .*" He retells this event in the first of the four sonnets concerned with his new love.

The other three sonnets are similarly "recapitulative." In the second sonnet he begins to speak in terms of the lady's beauty, of her pale "color of love and pity" (we may remember the "color of the pearl" attributed to Beatrice in the first canzone). In the third sonnet remorse sets in; he curses his eyes which, we learn for the first time, have ceased to weep and have begun to enjoy what they look upon. He is conscious, that is, of infidelity to Beatrice. But he blames his eyes not only for enjoying the sight of the lady, but also, and perhaps mainly, for having ceased to weep; and he reminds them that when they used to perform their function duly they were able to make all those who looked upon him weep. It is as if he can conceive of salvation from infidelity only in terms of a renewal of morbid self-pity. He warns his eyes that he will continuously remind them of Beatrice—because, as he said in the prose, the pity which he enjoys from the lady herself is inspired only by her regret for Beatrice. In the fourth sonnet he imagines a debate between the heart and the soul. The heart (or desire, as we are told in the prose) welcomes a "gentil pensero" that speaks of the new lady; the soul (or reason) is disturbed by the power of this thought which drives out all others. But the heart has the last word. We may remember that the author, in summing up the first nine years of the lover's devotion to Beatrice, allows him to claim that reason always ruled his love.

Love for Beatrice had been, for the protagonist, largely a source of self-pity, and this need for pity becomes the source of infidelity. It is as if with love of this self-centered kind it does not matter what direction the love takes; it is as if in his weak moments it was not Beatrice whom he loved. What he sought and what he loved was only a source of emotional self-indulgence. Thus, his infidelity was no more of a sin that had been the hysterical aspects of his fidelity to Beatrice. (That in the *Convivio* the "lady at the window" will become a symbol of the Lady Philosophy should not concern the reader of the *Vita nuova*: that Dante feels free to use earlier compositions to suit his purpose at the moment should already be clear.)

The struggle between the rational soul and the desirous heart which seemed to be leading toward the triumph of the heart is brought to a sudden end with the re-establishment of reason: one day his imagination is seized by the figure of Beatrice as he first saw her dressed in her crimson robes. He begins once more to think of her and, remembering her in "the sequence of past times," his heart, with pain, repents. With the impact of this inner movement through time he is shaken completely free of his recent infatuation, and all his thoughts return to Beatrice. He tells us of his sighs breathing her name; as they issue from his chastened heart they speak of what is the preoccupation of his heart: how she departed from us. With his allegiance to Beatrice sealed, he can weep once more, weep again and again until his eyes are encircled with a purplish color, being thus justly rewarded for their wantonness. And his painful thoughts often induce in him a near-cataleptic state.

The sonnet that follows, we are told, contains the "essence" (*sentenza*) of what has preceded. The first two quatrains are devoted to a description of his suffering eyes. The tercets, too, speak of pain:

> Questi penseri, e li sospir ch'eo gitto,
>   diventan ne lo cor sì angosciosi
>   ch'Amor vi tramortisce, sì lien dole;
>   però ch'elli hanno in lor li dolorosi
>   quel dolce nome di madonna scritto,
>   e de la morte sua molte parole.

(These meditations and the sighs I breathe
  become so anguishing within the heart
  that Love, who dwells there, faints, he is so tortured;
  for on those thoughts and sighs of lamentation
  the sweet name of my lady is inscribed,
  with many words relating to her death.)

The protagonist has been privileged to have a vision of Beatrice which has moved him to sincere repentance. He promises his reader to offer the true signficance of this experience in a sonnet—which, however, is devoted entirely to a description of his own suffering!

Thus, the lover in returning to Beatrice has returned to the sterile mood of helpless grief over her death. He has come home. The reappearance of Beatrice in his imagination was only a reminder of things past, an invitation to hug to himself once again the familiar feelings of self-pity. He sees his lady not as she has become: Beatrice in glory cherished by Heaven, a vision revealing new truth, inviting to movement forward, but as she was at the age of nine, on the day that set in motion the chain of debilitating emotional experiences. His thoughts, it is true, are not concentrated only upon the figure of the child Beatrice: after her first appearance in his imagination he begins remembering her "in the sequence of past times." The term "sequence" implies that he re-evokes, in order, all the scenes and all the moods that followed their first meeting (II). And it is quite possible that such a re-evocation moving forward in time to the present might well have afforded him a clearer vision of what his love for Beatrice should have been (it certainly is clear to the reader of the *Vita nuova*). But the forward movement through time does not extend to the present, it stops short at Beatrice's death: this, we are told, came to be the sole preoccupation of his heart ("how she departed from us"). He refuses to go beyond her death, to go beyond to the meaning of her death. And because ever since the actual death of Beatrice his attempts to go beyond had been few and brief, the only vision of her that was vouchsafed him was the memory of the earliest past. We have in Chapter XXIX a dreary *aria da capo*. The protagonist is imprisoned within the limits of beginning and (inorganic) ending.

In Chapter XL of the *Vita nuova* the lover apparently sees strangers for the first time. The narrow frame of his vision, concentrated upon himself and Beatrice, had been able, at best, to comprehend vague figures of Florentine friends and acquaintances, all of whom in one way or another had been associated with his love for Beatrice. Now he sees a group of pilgrims on their way to Rome passing through the middle of the city "where the most gracious lady was born, lived and died." They appear to him to be absorbed in their thoughts; they make on him the impression of having come from far away; they are alien, unfamiliar. He is reminded that there are other places in the world besides Florence where one may have his home.[21] He realizes also that these thoughtful strangers are not thinking about his suffering or even about the city of Florence suffering from the loss of Beatrice (they are not thinking "Quomodo sedit sola civitas . . ."); their thoughts must be on their own friends living in distant lands. He has a reaction of defiance: "If I had the opportunity, I could make them weep." And he decides to write a sonnet addressed to them.

Chapter XL ends with a pedantic note as Dante the "glossator" intervenes to list the three terms applicable to religious pilgrims: *peregrini, romei, palmieri*. And he offers, as it were, an apology for having applied the term *peregrini* to those who, being on their way to Rome, should have properly been called *romei*. If one should read these words without recognizing the intervention of the "glossator," one would not fail to have a very favorable opinion of the development of the protagonist's mood. He would seem to be passing, from an attitude of selfish resentment over the pilgrims' indifference, to a calmer, nobler mood, remembering the sacred goal of their pilgrimage, realizing that they are "pilgrims" not only in the general sense of being far away from home but also in the religious sense of being on their way to worship at a shrine. The protagonist's first feeling of pique would seem to have given way to the solemn realization that the pilgrims' spiritual goal is more important than his grief or that of the people of Florence; his provincialism which was like the social reflection of his self-centeredness would have given way to a recognition of new vistas.

But the poem that ends the chapter reveals the falsity of such an interpretation. Just as it is impossible to believe that Chapter XXIX, the "essay" on the number nine, represents the mood of the protagonist in the days following the death of Beatrice—his real mood being reflected in his tear-drenched third *canzone*—so we must refuse to attribute the dispassionate attitude revealed in the closing section of the chapter to the young lover who, having watched with surprise and resentment the pilgrims passing through and beyond his city, decides to write a poem in which he could pretend to make them weep (and forget their holy goal), and which, indeed, reveals no other concern.

The contrast between the protagonist of the *Vita nuova*, with his self-centeredness and provincialism, and the protagonist of the *Divine Comedy*, to whom the goal of the beatific vision soon comes to be the unique concern, is obvious. And the story of a young Florentine man of letters, moving through familiar streets, will give way to that of the pilgrim, Everyman, moving through the strange (and never before traveled by mortal man) topography of Hell, Purgatory and Paradise. Is it only a coincidence that the lover who, as protagonist of the *Divine Comedy*, will have the role of a pilgrim is first made aware of something alien to his ego by the appearance precisely of dedicated pilgrims?

The last poem of the *Vita nuova* describes the ascent of the lover's spirit to Heaven:

> *Oltre la spera che più larga gira*
> *passa 'l sospiro ch'esce del mio core:*
> *intelligenza nova, che l'Amore*
> *piangendo mette in lui, pur su lo tira.*
> *Quand'elli è giunto là dove disira,*
> *vede una donna, che riceve onore*
> *e luce sì, che per lo suo splendore*
> *lo peregrino spirito la mira.*
>
> *Vedela tal, che quando 'l mi ridice,*
> *io no lo intendo, sì parla sottile*
> *al cor dolente che lo fa parlare.*
> *So io che parla di quella gentile,*
> *però che spesso ricorda Beatrice,*
> *sì ch'io lo 'ntendo ben, donne mie care.*

> (Beyond the sphere that makes the widest round,
>   passes the sigh arisen from my heart;

a new intelligence that Love in tears
endowed it with is urging it on high.
Once arrived at the place of its desiring,
it sees a lady held in reverence,
splendid in light, and through her radiance
the pilgrim spirit looks upon her being.

But when it tries to tell me what it saw,
    I cannot understand the subtle words
it speaks to the sad heart that makes it speak.
    I know it tells of that most gracious one,
    for I often hear the name of Beatrice.
This much, at least, is clear to me, dear ladies.)[22]

We see the light of Beatrice shining in Heaven; we see her
light, we see the lover's spirit absorbed in looking at her. In
the first *canzone* the radiance of Beatrice on earth was sending
its rays toward Heaven; in the third, the full splendor of her
light moved from earth to Heaven; now it is shining steadily
into the eyes of a pilgrim spirit. But the glory of the quatrains
gives way to the bewilderment and disequilibrium of the tercets. For though this poem describes the ascent of the lover's
spirit to Heaven, this spirit is a sigh born of his longing: the
last of the twenty-two sighs that breathe through the *Vita
nuova*.[23] And though it is drawn above by the force of an "in-
telligenza nova," this "new intelligence" was inspired by Love
in tears; when the spirit returns to him with its message from
Beatrice, the lover is completely unable to understand it, for
it is the *grieving* heart that listens to it. Moreover, he himself
says in the preceding prose that the sonnet he decided to write
would be a description of his own condition ("lo quale narra
del mio stato").[24] In this sonnet where an old, stale theme still
lingers on, the light of Heaven also shines. But the meaning of
this brilliance is a mystery to our protagonist, a mystery which
will slowly begin to be clear only after the vision in the final

chapter (which the poet does not share with his reader), that inspires him to break off the "New Life":

Appresso questo sonetto apparve a me una mirabile visione, ne la quale io vidi cose che mi fecero proporre di non dire più di questa benedetta infino a tanto che io potesse più degnamente trattare di lei. E di venire a ciò io studio quanto posso, sì com'ella sae veracemente. Sì che, se piacere sarà di colui a cui tutte le cose vivono, che la mia vita duri per alquanti anni, io spero di dicer di lei quello che mai non fue detto d'alcuna. E poi piaccia a colui che è sire de la cortesia, che la mia anima se ne possa gire a vedere la gloria de la sua donna, cioè di quella benedetta Beatrice, la quale gloriosamente mira ne la faccia di colui qui est per omnia secula benedictus.

(After I wrote this sonnet there came to me a miraculous vision in which I saw things that made me resolve to say no more about this blessed one until I would be capable of writing about her in a nobler way. To achieve this I am striving as hard as I can, and this she truly knows. Accordingly, if it be the pleasure of Him through whom all things live that my life continue for a few more years, I hope to write of her that which has never been written of any other woman. And then may it please the One who is the Lord of graciousness that my soul ascend to behold the glory of its lady, that is, of that blessed Beatrice, who in glory contemplates the countenance of the One *qui est· per omnia secula benedictus.*)

Thus, in the final chapter of the *Vita nuova* Dante the Poet expresses his dissatisfaction with his protagonist, or, rather, he allows the protagonist to express his dissatisfaction with himself. As the result of a vision, which is not revealed to us, he decides to stop writing about Beatrice until he can do so more worthily.[25] The preceding visions that have come to him have made him decide to write; this one makes him decide to stop writing. Like the *Convivio*, then, the *Vita nuova* is an unfinished book. Unlike the *Convivio*, however, the *Vita nuova* is left unfinished for a positive, artistic purpose, and the decision to break off is announced as an event, the final event in the story itself. And, indeed, insofar as the action of the *Vita nuova* is to be seen as the development of the young Dante's love from preoccupation with his own feelings to enjoyment of Beatrice's excellence, in the direction of an exclusive concern with her heavenly attributes and with heavenly matters, then this action ends, in an important sense, in failure and in the recognition of failure.

*   *   *

In the first chapter of this essay was discussed the dual role of Dante the author of the *Vita nuova:* narrator and glossator-editor. But it is necessary to distinguish not only between these two auctorial roles but also between the author himself and the protagonist. In recent years the critics of the *Divine Comedy* have come to see more clearly the folly of confusing Dante the poet, the historical figure who wrote the poem and who occasionally speaks to the reader from out the poem in his own voice—and Dante the pilgrim, who is the poet's creation and who moves in a world entirely of the poet's invention. It has been some time since any critic has pointed to the prostrate figure of the pilgrim in Canto V of the *Inferno*, swooning in pity over Francesca's fate, as evidence that Dante himself, the poet-theologian who conceived and elaborated the grandiose plan of the *Divine Comedy*, was moved by tender compassion for the character he sent to Hell.

In the case of the *Vita nuova*, too, it is necessary to distinguish between the protagonist and the author, even if, in this text, the protagonist is himself a historical figure, and the world in which he moves is not purely fictitious. We must attempt to distinguish between the point of view of the youthful Dante who is the protagonist of the *Vita nuova,* and the point of view of the more mature Dante who is the narrator; that is, the critic must proceed as he would in the case of any first-person auto-biographical novel. He cannot take for granted that the point of view of the character undergoing various experiences in the past (the young lover swooning against the wall at the wedding feast in Chapter XIV of the *Vita nuova*) will be the same as that of his later self, who writes about the experiences in question some time after having lived through them, reflecting upon them in retrospect from a new perspective. How can we know just what the attitude was of the author of the *Vita nuova,* since, as has been said, he does not explicitly pass judgment on the protagonist's actions? Must it not be assumed that his would be the attitude not only of any mature person but also of one who knew that he was going to write a divine comedy?

What I have actually been trying to show is the fact that the more mature Dante is re-evoking his youthful experiences in a way to point up the folly, or the ignorance, of his younger self. We must imagine the poet, between the age of twenty-seven and thirty-five, as having already glimpsed the possibility of what was to be his terrible and grandiose masterpiece; we must imagine him rereading the love poems of his earlier years—a number of them, surely, with embarrassment. He would also have come to see Beatrice, too, as she was destined to appear in the *Divine Comedy,* and indeed, as she does appear briefly in the *Vita nuova:* in that essay (XXIX) on the miraculous quality of the number 9, which is the square of the number 3, that is of the Trinity, and which is Beatrice herself. Having arrived at this point, he would have chosen, then, several of his earlier love poems, including many that exhibit his younger self at his worst, in order to offer a warning example to other young lovers and especially to other love-poets. For, that some of the poems in the *Vita nuova* do represent the lover at his hysterical worst will become clear to anyone who reads through Dante's *Rime*. Though some of the poems in that collection reveal the lover's preoccupation with his own feelings and an insistence on the suffering he is enduring (attitudes characteristic of the love poetry of the time), in none of them is to be found the easy, puerile overflowing of grief that characterizes so many poems of the *Vita nuova*, or the desperate appeal, explicit or implicit, to the pity of others. And references to tears are almost entirely absent from the *Rime*.

That the exposure of Dante the protagonist was a constant (if not the only) preoccupation of Dante, the author of the *Vita nuova*, I am convinced. For if the picture the author presents of his youthful self had been offered for the reader's sympathy, the *Vita nuova* would have to be judged a very silly book indeed. And if other Dante scholars have arrived at a more idealistic, optimistic interpretation of the protagonist's development as a lover, I should say that there are two reasons for this. On the one hand, they have failed to distinguish clearly between the two Dantes: because, for example, in Chapter XXIX the true essence of Beatrice is clearly presented, many critics seem to have assumed that her true nature was perceived by the lover himself immediately after her death.[26] But the poems that follow all show that this could not possibly have been the case. Secondly, the critics have simply not read closely enough to catch the numerous indications of the lover's weaknesses and confusion that should be evident from the above analysis. It is understandable, given the confusion as to the two Dante's, attributing to the protagonist-lover, as they do, the clairvoyance of Dante the author, that the critics would tend to underestimate the significance of the many clear-cut demonstrations of failure: the failure of the protagonist to dominate his need for self-pity. What contempt Augustine, either as saint or as the lover he had been, would have felt for Dante's lover in the *Vita nuova!*

The *Vita nuova* is a cruel book. Cruel, that is, in the treatment of the human type represented by the protagonist. In the picture of the lover there is offered a condemnation of the vice of emotional self-indulgence and an exposure of its destructive effects on a man's integrity.[27] The "tender feelings" that move the lover to hope or to despair, to rejoice or to grieve (and perhaps to enjoy his grief), spring from his vulnerability and self-love; however idealistically inspired, these feelings cannot, except spasmodically, lead him ahead and above: as long as he continues to be at their mercy, he must always fall back into the helplessness of his self-centeredness. The sensitive man who would realize a man's destiny must ruthlessly cut out of his heart the canker at its center, the canker that the heart instinctively tends to cultivate.[28]

This is, I am convinced, the main, though not the only, message of the *Vita nuova*. And the consistent, uncompromising indictment it levels has no parallel in the literature of Dante's time—unless it be that baffling literary phenomenon which is the *Roman de la Rose*.[29] Of course, the *Vita nuova* offers more than a picture of the misguided lover: there is also the glory of Beatrice, and the slowly-increasing ability of the lover to understand it—who must confess at the end, however, that he has not truly understood it.

Both in the treatment of the lover and in that of Beatrice, Dante has gone far beyond what he found at hand in the love poetry of the Troubadours and of their followers. He has taken up two of their preoccupations (one might almost say obsessions) and developed each of them in a most original way: the lover's glorification of his own feelings, and his glorification of the Belovèd. Of the first he has made a caricature. Unlike his friend Cavalcanti, also highly critical of the havoc wrought by the emotions within a man's soul, who tends to make of his distraught lover a macabre portrait of doom, Dante has presented his protagonist again and again as a purely ridiculous figure, and more than once we have seen him mocked in society—the main scene being that of the wedding feast when the lover suffers a complete collapse in the presence of his lady. Such physiological manifestations of passion are familiar to us, of course, from the Troubadour love lyrics or the precepts of Andreas Capellanus (for instance, every lover regularly turns pale in the presence of his belovèd). What Dante has done with this conventional material is to stage it (we hear the lover's sobs, we see him stagger, we feel the pain in the left breast spreading as he falls back against the wall for support)—as indeed had been done before him by Chrétien de Troyes and the author of the *Énéas*. Their intention is obviously comic, as we well may assume that Dante's was.

In my analysis of Chapter II of the *Vita nuova* I stated that all the important themes to be developed in the book are already suggested in this opening chapter. A few pages later, in treating the thematic relationship between the narrative and the poems, I had occasion to mention the importance of the theme of mockery which, I suggested, works on more than one level. The attentive reader must have wondered why, if this theme were so important, nothing was said of it in the analysis of the chapter which opens the story. This was a deliberate omission on my part: I felt that to introduce the idea of Dante's mockery of his younger self at the very beginning of my essay would win little credence from the reader. But surely Dante the author of the *Vita nuova* was smiling when he introduced into this chapter the three *spiriti* (a triad which never appears again) who choose to express in solemn Latin their reaction to the sight of Beatrice—the climax being reached in the weeping lament of the "natural spirit" (the spirit of diges-

tion!): *Heu miser, quia frequenter impeditus ero deinceps!*[30]
According to one critic the Latin of the *spiriti* serves to establish a kind of transcendental level: in a sense, the words are "oracular."[31] What the third "oracle" is prophesying, of course, is the succession of spells of indigestion which will afflict the young lover throughout the course of his new life. So at the very beginning of the *Vita nuova* the author has given a most important hint (which was surely not lost on the medieval reader) as to the light in which so many of the protagonist's actions should be viewed.

As to the conventional theme of "glorification of the lady," all critics of the *Vita nuova* will admit that Dante carried his idealization to a point never reached before by any poet—and which no poet after him would ever quite attempt to reach. However blurred the lover's vision may be of the gracious, pure, feminine Beatrice—Dante the Poet, in Chapter XXIX, probes to the essence of her being and presents the coldness of her sublimity, the coldness, the sublimity, of the square of the number 3. Thus, the (tender) foolishness of the lover is intensified by contrast with the (icy) perfection of the Belovèd.[32] Her nature was destined to inspire not tender sentiments, and surely not weak tears, but only the stern resolution to strive for spiritual growth. (Tears the divine Beatrice could approve, but these should be only tears of deep contrition, as she herself will tell the Pilgrim in the *Divine Comedy*, when she first addresses him on top of the Mountain of Purgatory: the Pilgrim, overcome by the appearance of Beatrice, trembling as he had years before at his sudden awareness of the presence of Beatrice at the wedding feast, turns to Virgil for comfort as "il fantolin corre alla mamma / quando ha paura o quand' elli è afflitto" and, finding him gone, begins to weep. Beatrice, knowing the bitter tears of contrition he must shed—after confessing his failure to learn the meaning of her death, and before being washed in the waters of Lethe—rebukes him sternly for his childish tears: "Dante, perché Virgilio se ne vada / non pianger anco, non piangere ancora,/ ché pianger ti convien per altra spada.")

With a few exceptions, Dante's lyrical poems (and not only those contained in the *Vita nuova*) are not superior as works of art, in themselves, to those of Cavalcanti and Guinizelli—or of Bernard de Ventadorn and Arnault Daniel. The greatness of the *Vita nuova* lies, not in the poems included by their author in the work, but in the purpose which he forced them to serve. Certainly it represents the most original form of recantation in medieval literature—a recantation that takes the form of a re-enactment, from a new perspective, of the sin recanted.

Notes

to the Essay on
the *Vita Nuova*

I *Patterns*

✿ ✿ ✿ ✿ ✿ 1. I̲t̲ i̲s̲ natural that when the poem describes not the emotions inspired by the experience recounted in the narrative but the experience itself, the effect made by the poem on the reader of the *Vita nuova* is "recapitulative": in Chapter III the narrative describes the first coming of Love, and the poem contains many of the same details—as if the poem were repeating the prose. Actually, of course, both on the biographical plane and on that of the artistic fiction the composition of the poem has preceded that of the prose account. With both groups of poems we must account for three events: first, the happening itself which inspired the poem, then the act of writing the poem and, finally, the writing of the explanatory prose narrative.

2. As for the four times that the event "recapitulated" in the poem has been a vision, it would seem only natural that the protagonist would want to describe such unique events in verse. But two visions he does not recapitulate in verse: that of Beatrice in Chapter XXXIX, and the third coming of Love in Chapter XII. Certainly there are at least two reasons that he was not inspired to write a poem about the appearance of Beatrice in his memory as she had first appeared to him. There is nothing dramatic about this vision. No words are spoken.

There is no movement. Moreover, it was not the vision itself that he wished to describe to the world but the intensity of feeling that this vision provoked: his overwhelming remorse, and his renewed allegiance to the image of Beatrice. Now, the same reason could not apply to the vision in Chapter XII: on the one hand, the third appearance of Love is most dramatic and, on the other, the lover's reactions to it are not revealed to us. Just why this vision was not recounted in verse should become clear later on in the discussion of the four appearances of Love.

3. The *divisioni* of the *sonetto doppio* in Chapter VII contain an ambiguous hint of the correct interpretation of the poem: the author divides it into two parts, stressing the opening lines of the second part (that is, the central part of the poem) in which he speaks of his past joy. He says that these lines were written "con altro intendimento che le stremme parti del sonetto non mostrano." Now the opening lines of the sonnet refer to his grief, as do also the closing lines (one would think that this would call for a tripartite division): perhaps Dante is telling us that the joy he presents in the central portion as inspired by the absent screen-lady who has departed was actually inspired by his love for Beatrice.

Incidentally, in his *divisioni* of sonnet XXI it seems to me that Dante is reading into the first three lines (corresponding to the first two subsections of the first part) something that they could not possibly mean.

4. In two of the poems accompanied by *divisioni* the conceptual pattern is considerably at variance with the metrical: the two parts of *Venite a intender* . . . (XXXII) consist of two and twelve lines respectively; the two parts of *L'amaro lagrimar* . . . (XXXVII) consist of thirteen lines and one line respectively.

For a completely different explanation of the *divisioni*, see Aldo Vallone, *La prosa della "Vita Nuova,"* Florence, 1963, p. 31–32.

5. For a discussion of these and other patterns of numerical symmetry that have been discerned in the *Vita nuova* see Kenneth McKenzie, PMLA XVIII, 341–355. He mentions, for example, Federzoni's further fragmentation of the second schema (10 / 1 / 9 / 1 / 10): since between the first sonnet and the first canzone there are nine poems, he divides: 1 / 9 / 1 / 9 / 1 / 9 / 1. McKenzie dismissed Federzoni's schema as unimportant, but he does not show why this arrangement is without significance. The reason, of course, is that the justification for the splitting up of the first group of ten poems (1 / 9) and the last group of ten poems (9 / 1) is based on the theme of the first and last sonnets: they both describe visions. But there are other sonnets (and other poems not sonnets) that also describe visions, and only if all of them would show symmetrical distribution could this schema hold true. This is unfortunate because the pattern on the surface is certainly attractive symbolically.

6. The two literary compositions written in the course of the *Vita nuova* which Dante explicitly states he will withhold from the reader are the *serventese* written in praise of sixty ladies (IV), and the letter written to "li principi de la terra" about the death of Beatrice. Incidentally, there is also suppression within the patterns of additions: nine times Dante decides not to offer his reader the usual *divisioni*.

7. In spite of Dante's admission in the Proem that he will not list every detail found in his Book of Memory, Professor Singleton (*An Essay on the "Vita nuova,"* Cambridge 1958, p. 32) sees in the Proem a statement of Dante's intention to

limit his function, in reproducing the context of the Book of Memory, to that of mere copyist. He admits, however, that many times Dante transgresses this limitation. Accordingly, he distinguishes between two Dantes: the Dante who limits himself to the purely scribal program as supposedly outlined in the Proem, and the Dante who takes it upon himself to be "glossator" (Singleton does not consider the matter of "omissions"). His distinction between Dante the author serving a purely narrative function, and Dante the author functioning also as glossator is, in itself, surely legitimate.

According to J. B. Shaw (*Essays on the "Vita nuova,"* Princeton 1929, Ch. III), there are three Dantes to be considered in studying the *Vita nuova* (p. 79), and he discusses most dramatically the relationship between these three—in which the reader also becomes involved (81–82):

> As we begin to read the work we find that at one extreme of knowledge is Dante the author, who knows everything; at the other is the Dante of the poems, who knows nothing except the emotions he is expressing; between the extremes is the protagonist, the Dante of the prose narrative, who knows more than the Dante of the poems, but not as much as the reader, and far less than Dante the author, although here and there, in his desire to inform the reader, he seems to endow his hero with more knowledge than seems reasonably probable. By the time we have come to the sonnet "Amore e 'l cor gentil" in the twentieth chapter, we realize that the Dante of the poems has caught up with the protagonist and both of them with the reader, and the author alone is ahead; and when the book is finished the three Dantes are one in knowledge, having outstripped the reader, who is lagging somewhat and looking back to pick up information he may have missed.

I must confess that I, as a reader of Professor Shaw, am "lagging somewhat" in my comprehension of his meaning.

8. The first reason given by Dante for his decision to omit all reference to the details of Beatrice's death is rather ambiguously worded:

La prima è che ciò non è del presente proposito, se volemo guardare nel proemio che precede questo libello.

I have assumed that this reminder of the Proem was concerned particularly with the last words which serve to modify his proposed role of simple scribe (*se non tutte, almeno la loro sentenzia*); and I have suggested that since the significance of Beatrice's death had already been made evident in the prophetic vision of Chapter XXIII, there was no need to offer the reader factual details involved in this event.

Shaw, however (op. cit., Ch. VI), evidently thinking in terms of Dante's overall presentation of himself as a faithful scribe, offers a quite different explanation. He believes that the death of Beatrice was not contained in Dante's Book of Memory: "He is utterly without memory of the event itself . . . It is not only that her death happens so suddenly that he knew nothing of it at the time, but it also so stunned him that he had no memory of his sensations on hearing the news." Singleton, on the other hand, cannot believe that Dante was ignorant of the details of Beatrice's death or that his memory had been affected by the shock (and he gives several reasons in support of this belief). If he refuses to discuss this important event and refers us to the Proem it is because, so Singleton believes, in the Proem Dante had promised to limit himself to the role of scribe. And Singleton continues: "To write here and now [?] of anything at all is simply not according to that intention; and it is one which he expects his reader to respect." But it is difficult for me to understand how Dante would be departing from his function of scribe in describing the death of Beatrice. And even if such a departure would be involved, the reader could hardly "respect his intention" since in the immediately following chapter (as Singleton himself admits with no qualms) he turns pure glossator in his discussion of the number 9. However, I agree with Singleton that we have no right to assume that Beatrice's death was not contained in the lover's Book of Memory.

9. Another suggestion, a most delicate suggestion, that the ladies in Chapter XVIII are gathered together out-of-doors, against a background of Nature, is offered by a simile drawn from Nature. After the lover has told the ladies that, having lost Beatrice's greeting, he has now placed his beatitude in something that cannot fail him, they respond to his remark with a flow of words and sighs which remind him of the fall of rain mingled with beautiful flakes of snow: "Allora queste donne cominciaro a parlare tra loro e sì come talora vedemo cadere l'acqua mischiate di bella neve, così, mi parea udire le loro parole uscire mischiate di sospiri."

10. There are eight groups of persons whom we see on stage with the protagonist: the two older ladies flanking Beatrice (III); the group of ladies at the wake of Beatrice's friend (VIII); the guests at the wedding feast (XIV); the ladies with whom he converses about his love (XVIII); those who return mourning from Beatrice's home (XXII); the masses who rush to see Beatrice pass (XXVI); the men who watch him drawing an angel and to whom he speaks (XXXIV); the pilgrims passing through the center of his city (XL). In one case we learn of the presence of a group of persons with whom he has been mingling, only after he leaves their company: Chapter XII opens with the statement that when Beatrice refused him her greeting as she passed, "mi giunse tanto dolore . . . che, *partito me da le genti*, in solingo parte andai. . . ."

11. Though the word *fratello* is not used of Beatrice's brother (XXXII) or *sorella* of Dante's sister (XXXIII), we do find Beatrice's father (XXII) called, secondarily, *lo suo padre*. After presenting him at the beginning of the chapter as "colui che era stato genitore di tanta maraviglia quanta si vedea ch'era questa nobilissima Beatrice," the author briefly touches upon the intimacy of the bond between father and child: "Onde, con ciò sia cosa che . . . nulla sia sì intima amistade come da buon padre a buon figliuolo e da buon figliuolo a buon padre. . . ." After this general statement (note that Dante permits himself to use the diminutive of the noun *figlio*) containing the word *padre* used generically, we find it at last applied to Beatrice's own father: ". . . e lo suo padre . . . fosse bono in alto grado. . . ."

12. Luigi Russo (as quoted by Pino da Prati, *Realtà e allegoria nella "Vita Nuova" di Dante*, 1963, p. 4) shows himself sensitive to the shadowy atmosphere in which the "real" events of the story unfold, but he has not seen the contrast between the presentation of these events and the colorful description offered in the visions; he sees, instead, a continuous flow within the same dream world.

II *Aspects*

1. In two cases (III and XII) Love appears to the protagonist in his sleep, and both times the experience is termed a *visione;* in Chapters IX and XXIV, where the word *imaginazione* is used, it is the lover's fancy while he is awake that conjures up the figure of Love. For purposes of convenience I shall often use the term "vision" in referring to all four scenes.

2. In addition to the scenes in Chapters III, IX, XII and XXIV, there are three other occasions in which Love speaks to the protagonist: in Chapter XV he warns him to flee the sight of Beatrice if he would not perish; in Chapter XXXIV he tells the lover's sighs to go forth (he actually addresses the *sospiri*); in Chapter XXIII, in the *canzone* prophesying the death of Beatrice, Love, after the angels have sung their hosannas, directs the lover to go look upon his lady. But in none of the three is the figure of Love visible. Again, in the first *canzone* (XIX) we hear Love speak and we see him gaze upon Beatrice, but he does not speak to the protagonist and no moment in time is fixed. In the first sonnet of Chapter VIII Love weeps and looks up toward Heaven, but he does not speak, and again the temporal reference is very vague. And in none of these scenes is Love the central figure.

In the five passages just mentioned there is at least some degree of what might be called "dramatic" personification. Then there are dozens of cases of a nondramatic nature in which some degree of personification is involved: of the more than 150 occurrences of the word *amore* in the *Vita nuova* there are only a few in which personification is totally excluded, as, for example, *questa donna era schermo di tanto amore* (VI). Usually the language and the constructions are such as to permit an interpretation of abstract personification to some degree: . . . *e ha lasciato amor meco dolente* (XXXI), *Sì lungiamente m'ha tenuto amore* . . . (XXVII), . . . *per la volontade d'amore* (IV).

3. I once believed that Dante's statement about the poet's need to be able to retell in prose what he had put into verse contained an explanation of his procedure of accompanying most of his poems with *divisioni* in prose. Compare his use of *aprire* in the first quotation from Chapter XXV (". . . con ragione la quale poi sia possible *d'aprire per prosa*") with his

explanation in Chapter XIV of the purpose of his *divisioni:* ". . . la divisione non si fa se non *per aprire* la sentenzia de la cosa divisa." But I have come to reject this idea, for the statements quoted above from Chapter XXV should mean, within the context of this chapter, that the poet would be able by means of a prose rewording to justify his use of poetic license. Yet never do we find in Dante's *divisioni* any attempt to rephrase the metaphorical in nonmetaphorical terms.

4. I know of no critic of the *Vita nuova* who has offered a detailed treatment of the appearances of the figure of Love. Shaw, for example, who believes that the significance of this figure changes in the course of the narrative, states that in his first two appearances (III and IX) he represents Cavalcantian love and in the last two (XII and XXIV) Guinizellian love; Singleton, who believes that the figure continues unchanged, declares him to be the Troubadour god of Love. But neither scholar attempts to show how all the details of the four scenes serve to support his theory.

5. Of the four visions described in the prose narrative of Chapters III, IX, XII, and XXIV, three are retold (III, IX and XXIV) in a sonnet following the prose; in Chapter XII the *ballata* that closes the chapter contains no allusion to the vision. In discussing the other three visions I shall limit myself almost entirely to the prose version. Hardly ever is a significant detail added in the sonnets; always some details of the prose version are absent. In fact, in the poem of Chapter XXIV the theological significance of the vision is entirely lacking.

6. Singleton, in an article devoted to the appearance of Love in Chapter XII (*Romanic Review* XXXVI, 89–102), believing that the vision in question is prophetic of Beatrice's death, says that Love weeps because he knows that Beatrice is soon to die. Shaw, replying to Singleton's article (*Italica* XXIV, 113–118),

states that Love's tears are due to his grief over Beatrice's refusal of her greeting, a refusal caused by her mistrust of the
protagonist's love.

If my interpretation of Love's significance in this scene is
correct, then the explanation of Shaw would be impossible; by
offering such a motivation for Love's tears, he would be identifying this figure with what I have called the Lesser Aspect. As
for Singleton's explanation, I should say that, even if the vision
were prophetic of Beatrice's death (which I do not believe),
tears over the approaching death and apotheosis of Beatrice
would be a reaction most unfitting the Greater Aspect of love
for Beatrice. How could this god, who in Chapter XXIV
compares Beatrice to Christ, weep at the thought of Beatrice
in glory?

Singleton, it is true, believes that Love in all of his appearances represents the Troubadour god of Love. And, in that
case, tears over the lady's death might be appropriate for such
a deity. But to identify with this deity the figure who appears
in Chapter XII is in my opinion impossible: the idea of the
Troubadour god of Love speaking solemn Latin is incongruous. Moreover, in Provençal love poetry the god of Love was
never dramatically personified. The *canso* (XVI) of Arnault
Daniel cited by Pignatelli as a possible influence on Dante's
personification of Love ("*La Vita nuova*" *di Dante*, Padova,
1949, p. 27) is hardly a case in point: the Provençal poet
merely states that Love commands him to serve his lady faith-
fully, and then devotes two stanzas to direct discourse supposedly representing the words of Love. But the figure of the
god does not appear on stage, and there is no dialogue.

7. Singleton believes that in Love's self-definition involving
a contrast with the lover, the god is proclaiming his ability and
the lover's inability to see the future—that is, Love can see
ahead to Beatrice's death and the lover cannot. It is true that

when this image was applied to the Christian God by theologians (compare, for example, Thomas Aquinas, Bonaventure, Duns Scotus), the center of the circle was taken to represent eternity, equidistant from all the points on the circumference, in the sense that, in Eternity, present, past and future can be seen as one. But that this metaphor was intended to stress God's ability to know the future, as representing the divine attribute *par excellence*, is less certain, as Shaw points out in his answer to Singleton. And even if such were the emphasis, it seems out of proportion for Love to use such a sublime image in order merely to claim that he is able to foresee the death of a given individual, while the lover is not. Shaw, who shares my opinion that the vision in question is not prophetic, believes, as I do, that the metaphor, and the contrast between the god and the lover, have to do with the two types of love these represent. I must confess, however, that I was not able to grasp the precise nature of the contrast intended by Shaw.

8. The color of the cloth in which Beatrice's body is wrapped (III), and which is probably meant to suggest her shroud, recalls that of the garment she wore when the protagonist first saw her in the preceding chapter. And perhaps the white of the garment she wore when she first greeted the lover is reflected in another vision, in which Love does not appear: in the lover's prophetic dream of Beatrice's death he sees her face being covered by a white veil. Thus the colors of *caritas* and purity appear twice in the *Vita nuova:* once in the narrative proper, once in visions.

9. The four visions in which Love appears on stage and speaks to the protagonist have been analyzed from the point of view of the Greater or Lesser Aspect. Each of these two aspects is represented in three of the four visions (during the whole of it, or a part of it).

One must wonder about the distribution of roles in the five cases mentioned (Note 1) of partial dramatic personification of Love. In two of these it is possible to imagine that the Greater Aspect is represented (in the first *canzone* when Love marvels at Beatrice's perfection, and in the central *canzone* when he bids the lover go look upon his lady dead), but because of the brevity of the god's intervention, it is difficult to be sure that this is the case. In the other three, however, it is clear that we have to do with the Lesser Aspect: the Greater Love would hardly weep at the death of one called to glory (VIII); and it could only be the Lesser Love that would urge the lover to protect himself by fleeing the sight of Beatrice (XV), or invite him to give free rein to his sighs in grieving over Beatrice's death (XXXIV).

And, as for the dozens of cases of minimal personification in which the lover speaks of "love" and its effects, it is probably the Greater Love that goes with Beatrice when she passes before the people to freeze the hearts of the wicked. But in all the other cases we find either colorless, inconsequential allusions to the god or else clear representation of the Lesser Aspect, the most frequent being the destruction wrought by Love on the lover's faculties. One might have thought that after Chapter XXIV, when he experienced complete fusion with the Greater Love, some traces of this experience might be found in his thoughts about love. Actually, it is from Chapter XXIV on that we find the Lesser Love most frequently involved: in fact, it is Love, the protagonist tells us, who sets the stage for his infidelity to Beatrice.

10. The word *L'altrier* 'the other day' in the opening line of the sonnet in Chapter IX (*Cavalcando l'altrier per un cammino* is a Provençalism used fairly frequently by the Italian poets. Indeed, the opening line itself is reminiscent of the Provençal *pastorella*—compare the one by Gui d'Ussel which

begins: *L'altrier cavalcava*. Why should Dante choose to remind us of this genre in a poem which has nothing to do with an amorous encounter between a man and a peasant girl? Whereas popular love poetry in general treats of natural sensuous love, the *pastorella* in its most characteristic form treated this love at its crudest: what was sought by the "lover" was simply the act of coitus. And instead of the tenderness so characteristic of the *alba*, for instance, there is usually present a note of cynicism. What more fitting than that the reader should be reminded of this ignoble treatment of love in a chapter devoted exclusively to the figure of the Lesser Aspect of Love (this contains the only vision concerned with this Aspect alone) who, here, is encouraging the lover in his amorous subterfuges.

11. Whatever be the precise symbolic significance of the scene in Chapter III in which the lady is forced to eat the heart of the lover, it surely owes nothing to the wide-spread medieval "legend of the eaten heart"—a connection proposed by D'Ancona in *Scritti danteschi* (277 ff.). In all the versions of that legend contained in Matzke's collection ("The Legend of the Eaten Heart" in *MLN* XXVI, 1–8) a vindictive husband takes revenge on his faithless wife by offering her, as a delicacy for the palate, the heart of her lover. That the theme concerned with a husband's sadistic revenge on an adulterous wife could have inspired the scene in the *Vita nuova* is impossible. D'Ancona, it is true, also mentions other tales concerned with the ultimate disposal of a human heart (one can only wonder why he brings in the eating of a dead hero's heart by warriors, or the feeding of a cruel lady's heart to dogs), but it is the theme of a lady being forced to eat her lover's heart unwittingly which he thinks Dante has seized upon in order to give it allegorical meaning. Here, supposedly, the eating of the heart would amount to an "interpenetration" (a one way inter-

penetration?) involving the concept "two hearts in a single breast." But to allegorize a theme is to give greater depth to a significance already present in the original—not to transform this significance beyond recognition.

If one should attempt to discuss the many differences that separate the legend in question from the first mysterious dream in the *Vita nuova*, the result would sound like a nightmare of confusion. This is often the result of attempting to refute in detail a theory which should never have been proposed in the first place.

12. Because Love in his final appearance in Chapter XXIV speaks from the lover's heart—or, as we are also told, the lover's heart speaks using Love's tongue—he will not speak in Latin, as he had done in his two earlier appearances (he does not, however, miss the opportunity to quote from Latin: "Ego vox clamantis . . ."). Thus, it could be said that Love as the Greater Aspect always speaks in Latin when he is separate from the lover.

Incidentally, the perfect fusion of the god of Love and the lover that takes place almost immediately at the beginning of the vision has been anticipated in Chapter IX by the perfect fusion which takes place at the end of the vision as Love seems to become a part of the lover himself—as if he had disappeared into him. But then it was the Lesser Love who entered into the fusion. Thus, a similarity of detail between the two scenes makes for the greatest of contrasts between them: in Chapter IX the lover was wholly given up to Lesser Love; in Chapter XXIV he is wholly given up to Perfect Love.

13. The pattern of "three" is occasionally found in the *divisioni*, but these may also be divided into four, or five, or two parts, the latter being the more frequent. Incidentally, though it is legitimate to speak of "the three *canzoni*" of the *Vita nuova*, one should not forget the imperfect *canzone* of two

stanzas written on behalf of Beatrice's brother, or the *canzone* which the lover began, only to be interrupted after one stanza by the news of Beatrice's death. The "threeness" of the *canzoni* is, in this way, somewhat blurred.

14. And it could be said that the living Beatrice of the story splits into two: she is not only the walking miracle of purifying efficacy, the sanctifying grace of the *Vita nuova*, she is also very much a lady of the world who, miffed at the report of her admirer's attentions to another lady, refuses to give him her greeting, and who, seeing his lovesick appearance at a social gathering, does not hesitate to join in the general derision.

15. At the beginning of the discussion of the surprising frequency of "pairs" in the *Vita nuova* it was said, as something obvious, that the number two has no Christian symbolic value (as do the numbers three and ten). But of course it has a philosophical symbolic value, cf. H. Flanders Dunbar, *Symbolism in Medieval Thought* . . . (Yale University Press, 1929), p. 502: "The significance of One in religion and in philosophy is clear, in the persistent strivings of the human mind for monotheism and for monism. *Two expresses the fundamental dualities of the universe, which make monism and monotheism alike seem so beset with contradictions.*" As for the figure of Love it should, of course, have been a One, the Greater Aspect alone; we have seen the many "contradictions with which it has been beset."

III *Growth*

1. The forty-two chapters of the *Vita nuova* must be divided into two main parts: that preceding and that following the death of Beatrice (I–XXVII; XXVIII–XLII). The first half can also be divided into two parts (I–

XVI; XVII–XXVII), the second beginning with Dante's rejection of self-centeredness and his choice of a new theme: praise of his lady.

2. The poem of mourning for the first screen-lady begins with a paraphrase of Lamentations I, 12: "O vos qui transitis per viam. . . ." This invitation to the passerby to stop and mediate upon the grief of Jerusalem is changed by the poet into an appeal to the pilgrims of love": "O voi che per la via d'amore passate. . . ." The moving words of Jeremiah were supposed to represent the lament expressed by the city itself, destroyed and desolate, pleading for the compassion of mankind. And this sublime picture of historic grief the lover was able to exploit in his attempt to deceive others with his mock love-lament.

3. In Chapter X the wave of gossip that destroyed the lover's happiness is represented as a single voice: "questa soverchievole voce." We are reminded here of the theme of the *lausengiers* in Provençal poetry, those persons who loved to spy upon lovers, reveal their secrets, and even indulge in calumny—all this because they are inherently incapable of understanding the love that springs from the "gentle heart." They are the enemies of love and *joi*. In the love poetry of the Troubadours they play only seldom a dramatic role; they represent mainly a possibility forever to be dreaded. Here in the *Vita nuova*, however, they are a strong dramatic force, producing irrevocable consequences.

4. The summary of events recorded in the climactic Chapter X is offered, somehow, from a distance. The reader feels the increasing spread and virulence of the gossip which finally reaches the ears of Beatrice, who straightway refuses her greeting. But what lay behind Beatrice's refusal could not have been

clear to the lover at the moment she passed him by and, in fact, he is made to learn it two chapters later, when Love explains the reason for Beatrice's hostility. Thus, Dante the author of the *Vita nuova* anticipates in Chapter X what the protagonist learns only later.

5. Chapter XII, which contains the artfully delayed description of the lover's bitter reaction to Beatrice's refusal of her greeting in Chapter X, opens with the words, "Ora tornando al proposito . . .". Singleton (*Essay* . . . p. 34) interprets these words as a confession on the author's part of having wandered from the story in Chapter XI. Feigning surprise that the description of Beatrice's greeting could constitute a "digression," Singleton explains this digression as follows:

> Why was it a digression from the "subject" to describe the effects of Beatrice's greeting when anything at all connected with Beatrice would seem to be of the essence of his subject? Because this chapter XI is a chapter written *now* by the scribe, written now and in the present tense, as the reader will note, and hence not according to the intention declared in the Proem.
>
> Chapter XXIX on the number nine is just a digression, too.

But what the reader will surely note is that Chapter XI is *not* written in the present tense; describing as it does habitual activity in the past, it is written throughout in the imperfect tense (that is, after the introductory *Dico che* . . .).

In the notes to her translation of the *Vita nuova* (Penguin Press, 1969) Barbara Reynolds (p. 109) also considers Chapter XI to be a digression. The reason she offers I find equally incomprehensible.

6. There is only one full-fledged simile in the *Vita nuova:* that in Chapter XVIII mentioned earlier:

> *Allora queste donne cominciaro a parlare tra loro, e sì come talora vedemo cadere l'acqua mischiata di bella neve, così mi parea udire le loro parole uscire mischiate di sospiri.*

We note the conventional structure *sì come . . . così . . .* and the perfect (if chiastic!) paralleling of A and B. Both of these features are lacking in the simile of Chapter XII where, after a reference to his spell of weeping, the protagonist states that he went to his room:

> *. . . e quivi, chiamando misericordia a la donna de la cortesia, e dicendo "Amore, aiuta lo tuo fedele," m'addormentai* come un pargoletto battuto lagrimando.

Nevertheless, this everyday, yet colorful simile is surely intended to strike the reader's attention—and to suggest a contrast with the more elaborate simile of Chapter XVIII where the lover, no longer in a childish mood, will be inspired to choose the new theme of praise. The few other partial similes found in the *Vita nuova* are rather nondescript; only these two stand out, offering, almost, an additional "set of two's": the one reflecting the Lesser Aspect, the other the program of praise which, of course, points in the direction of the Greater Aspect. It is fitting that the first should be an imperfect simile.

7. The majority of scholars see in the last two lines of the second stanza of the first *canzone* ("E che dirà ne lo inferno: 'O mal nati, / io vidi la speranza dei beati.'") an allusion to the *Divine Comedy*, of which Dante would already have had some preliminary conception. And it may be noted that the phrase *mal nati* is used to refer to the damned in Canto V of the *Inferno*, when they are first presented, undergoing the judgment of Minòs. A number of critics, however, believe these lines to be a reference to the poet's possible damnation: a similar intimation of damnation, involving a similar memory of his happiness on earth with his lady, is found among the *Rime* (*Lo do-*

loroso amor). Still other scholars have seen in the phrase *ne lo inferno* merely a reference to the desolation of Florence after the death of Beatrice. The last explanation is not convincing, and the second is preposterous.

Among those who see in these lines an allusion to Dante's *magnum opus,* some believe that the second stanza was added much later. More likely would be the supposition that the entire *canzone* was written some time after his youthful period.

8. The picture of the kindling of love in the heart of the beholder, which is contained in the last stanza of the first *canzone,* differs from the traditional one in that there are involved not only the eyes of the one who beholds the beautiful lady, but also the eyes of the lady herself, from which issue the flaming spirits that strike the eyes of him who looks upon her, and pass to his heart.

9. Cavalcanti's poems of praise are the three sonnets:

I
Biltà di donna e di saccente core
e cavalieri armati che sien genti;
cantar d'augelli e ragionar d'amore;
adorni legni 'n mar forte correnti;

aria serena quand' apar l'albore
e bianca neve scender senza venti;
rivera d'acqua e prato d'ogni fiore;
oro, argento, azzuro 'n ornamenti:

ciò passa la beltate e la valenza
de la mia donna e 'l su' gentil coraggio,
sì che rasembra vile a che ciò guarda;

e tanto più d'ogn' altr' ha canoscenza,
quanto lo ciel de la terra è maggio.
A simil di natura ben non tarda.

II

Avete 'n vo' li fior' e la verdura
e ciò che luce od è bello a vedere;
risplende più che sol vostra figura:
chi vo' non vede, ma' non pò valere.

In questo mondo non ha creatura
sì piena di bieltà né di piacere;
e chi d'amor si teme, lu' assicura
vostro bel vis' a tanto 'n sé volere.

Le donne che vi fanno compagnia
assa' mi piaccion per lo vostro amore;
ed i' le prego per lor cortesia

che qual più può più vi faccia onore
ed aggia cara vostra segnoria,
perché di tutte siete la migliore.

III

Chi è questa che vèn, ch'ogn'om la mira,
che fa tremar di chiaritate l'âre
e mena seco Amor, sì che parlare
null' omo pote, ma ciascun sospira?

O deo, che sembra quando li occhi gira,
dical' Amor, ch'i' nol savria contare:
cotanto d'umilità donna mi pare,
ch'ogn'altra ver' di lei i' la chiam' ira.

Non si poria contar la sua piagenza,
ch'a le' s'inchin' ogni gentil vertute,
e la beltate per sua dea la mostra.

Non fu sì alta già la mente nostra
e non si pose 'n noi tanta salute,
che propiamente n'aviàn canoscenza.

With Guinizelli we find the two sonnets:

I

Io voglio del ver la mia donna laudare
ed asembrali la rosa e lo giglio:

più che stella dìana splende e pare,
e ciò ch'è lassù bello a lei somiglio.

Verde river' a lei rasembro e l'âre,
tutti color di fior', giano e vermiglio,
oro ed azzurro e ricche gioi per dare:
medesmo Amor per lei rafina meglio.

Passa per via adorna, e sì gentile
ch'abassa orgolio a cui dona salute,
e fa 'l de nostra fé se non la crede;

e no·lle pò appressare om che sia vile;
ancor ve dirò c'ha maggior vertute:
null' om pò mal pensar fin che la vede.

II
Gentil donzella, di pregio nomata,
degna di laude e di tutto onore,
ché par de voi non fu ancora nata
né sì compiuta di tutto valore,

pare che 'n voi dimori onne fíata
la deítà de l'alto deo d'amore;
de tutto compimento siete ornata
[e] d'adornezze e di tutto bellore:

ché 'l vostro viso dà sì gran lumera
che non è donna ch'aggia in sé beltate
ch'a voi davante non s'ascuri in cera;

per voi tutte bellezze so' afinate,
e ciascun fior fiorisce in sua manera
lo giorno quando vo' vi dimostrate.

10. In interpreting the unfinished *canzone* as evidence of the breakdown of the lover's program of praise, because of its position immediately following the poems of praise, I admitted that, actually, it might have been composed much earlier. But how could we account for the existence of an earlier poem of just one stanza (though fourteen lines in length, it does not have the usual form of the sonnet)? Perhaps the young Dante

had begun a *canzone* that was interrupted by some other event than the one he gives as reason for his failure to conclude it. Or he may have attempted the experiment of a one-stanza *canzone:* Chapter XXXIII contains a *canzone* of two stanzas. This may remind us of the sonnet with two beginnings in Chapter XXXIV: there, the normal limits of the genre have been extended; in Chapter XXXIII they have been reduced. The last two cases, at least, must reflect Dante's delight in experimenting with breaking the rules of the metrical game. Such experiments (slightly reminiscent of the Provençal *descort*) do not appear in any other poems of Dante outside the *Vita nuova*.

11. In Chapter XXX, discussing the letter written to the princes of the land about the desolation of Florence caused by Beatrice's death, Dante refers, in passing, to the poems that will follow as his "new material":

> Poi che fue partita da questo secolo . . . io . . . scrissi a li principi de la terra alquanto de la sua condizione, pigliando quello cominciamento di Geremia profeta che dice: Quomodo sedet sola civitas. E questo dico, acciò che altri non si maravigli perchè io l'abbia allegato di sopra [i.e. Chapter XXVIII] quasi come entrata de la nuova materia che appresso vene.

Dante may have believed at this point that he would be able to write poems of deeper praise for Beatrice; or, as many of the commentators seem to believe, he may have used the expression *nuova materia* to refer to the replacement of the theme of praise by that of grief over Beatrice's death.

12. When in Chapter XVII the protagonist decided to write no more poems concerned with the state of his feelings, he did not speak of being ashamed of what he had written. It is rather as if he were exhausted by the emotional tension that had gone into the writing of his last four sonnets, and had come to realize the futility of continuing along the same lines. But in

Chapter XVIII, after he had been forced to announce his new theme and had been reminded by the lady of the difference between this and his earlier theme, he knew shame for the first time.

13. Chapter XVIII, describing the lover's meeting with his sarcastic Muse, offers a second scene of mockery to be found in the *Vita nuova*. The first event (the scene at the wedding feast) had also inspired him to write a poem, but it was one of a very different nature: the whimpering sonnet rebuking Beatrice, "Con l' altre donne mia vista gabbate."

14. The critics who stress the spontaneous inspiration of the opening line of the first *canzone* (XIX), as if forgetting about the poetic straits in which the protagonist had previously found himself (XVIII), are probably thinking in terms of another book—remembering the conversation between Bonagiunta and the pilgrim in *Purgatory* XXIV. Having recognized the visitor to his terrace as the author of "Donne ch'avete intelletto d'amore," Bonagiunta elicits from him the famous definition of his manner of poetic composition ("Io mi son un che . . .") which, supposedly, stresses its artlessness (an artlessness which critics have, in turn, ascribed to the whole so-called school of the *dolce stilnovisti;* but see my article "Le ali di Dante. . . ," *Convivium* XXXIV [1966], 361–368).

15. The coincidences involved in Dante's inspiration to compose his poems of praise have been seen by Luigi Pietrobono (*Saggi danteschi* [Torino, 1954], p. 9 seq.), and by Fausto Montanari (*L'esperienza poetica di Dante* [Florence, 1968], pp. 74–5). Both seem to believe that his inspiration was ultimately willed by God; Montanari, however, is at the same time capable of seeing, in the conversation between the lover and the ladies, a verbal contest such as was apparently characteristic of courtly conversation.

16. It might be said that the sternness of Beatrice's figure in the mid-stanza of the first *canzone* has already begun to be dissolved in stanza IV, which describes her effect on the beholder only in terms of the love she inspires; the stanza ends with an appeal to the ladies to whom his poem is addressed. And the last stanza, as we know, brings us back into the atmosphere of courtly society with which the *canzone* opens (the author seems to return to this atmosphere with a sense of relief). Surely the first and last stanzas offer an incongruous framework for the poem whose essence lies in the three central stanzas—of a sublimity never to be attained again in the *Vita nuova*.

17. Within the repetitious sonnets of praise we may also note a development away from the awesome. Whereas the first sonnet (like the first *canzone*) presents Beatrice as moving in unlimited space, passing as it were before mankind, in the last two we are forced by the preceding prose section to think of a Florentine background, as Dante insists on the local truth of the citizens' veneration for Beatrice—they rush to see her pass.

18. The first of the Troubadours, William of Aquitaine, offers, in the central stanzas (IV, V) of the *canso* "Mout jauzens me prenc en amar", an unforgetable picture of his lady's ability to transform all who come in contact with her:

> *Totz joys li deu humiliar,*
> *e tota ricor obezir*
> *mi dons, per son belh aculhir,*
> *e deu son belh plazent esguar;*
> *e deu hom mais cent ans durar*
> *qui·l joy de s'amor pot sazir.*
>
> *Per son joy pot malautz sanar,*
> *e per sa ira sas morir*
> *e savis hom enfolezir*

e belhs hom sa beutat mudar
e·l plus cortes vilanejar
e totz vilas encortezir.

Hers, surely, is a superhuman power. But inserted between the first and last lines of stanza V is a picture of capricious, even sinister forces at work. The same lady who can heal and ennoble a man may also exert on him the power of Circe.

19. There is a logical justification of a sort for the poet's following up the sonnets of praise in Chapters XXI and XXVI with a poem about his own feelings; this would be in line with a comparable modification of theme begun in Chapter XXI. There he had shifted from the generic description of the effect of any lady's beauty on any man (described in Chapter XX) to the effect of the beauty of the particular individual Beatrice on whoever might observe her, and, in Chapter XXVI, on the citizens of Florence; to shift now to her effect on him, personally, represents a similar narrowing of focus.

But it is not only the choice of theme but the sickly treatment of it that mars the poem.

20. Dante's vision of the death of Beatrice with details suggestive of the Crucifixion is the dramatic high point of the *Vita nuova*. This vision was induced by a severe illness that had overtaken him; his physical condition leads him to think of his own mortality, which in turn brings him to the realization that one day Beatrice too must die. And he seems to see the faces of ladies wild with wrath and hear them chant "You are going to die!" He hears laments of mourning uttered by strange dishevelled women, and then begins to witness the dreadful portents of Beatrice's death. But it is difficult to see just what this magnificent evocation of phantasmagoric images reveals of the stage reached in the spiritual progress of the pro-

tagonist. On the one hand the Christ-like nature of Beatrice is suggested (in the macabre details presented): on the other the poem is the product of illness, morbidity and delirium.

Shaw in his *Essays* . . . devotes almost all of Chapter V to this vision, being mainly interested in a comparison between the narrative and the poem that follows. I cannot accept all the details of Shaw's treatment, and I should say that his approach is vitiated from the start by his conviction that the narrative was intended as a commentary on and a retouching of the poem written sometime earlier (in fact, he suggests it was written exactly one year earlier).

The most unacceptable of his proposals is his interpretation of line 13 of the third stanza of the *canzone:* "visi di donne m'apparver crucciati". He sees in this line a reference (for which there is no exact parallel in the prose) to women who are jealous of Beatrice. Not only is there no indication in all of the *Vita nuova* that such a jealousy existed, but in the last sonnet of praise (XXVI) such a possibility is excluded:

> *E sua bieltate è di tanta virtute,*
> *che nulla invidia a l'altre ne procede,*
> *anzi le face andar seco vestute*
> *di gentilezza, d'amore e di fede;*
> *La vista sua fa ogni cosa umile.*

21. Twice (IX and XIX) we learn of Dante's departure from Florence, but the place to which he goes is not mentioned. It is as if he conceives of travel to another place in terms only of absence from Florence. The other places themselves do not exist as such.

22. The last poem in the *Vita nuova* is addressed, as we learn only in the last line, to "my dear ladies." The line ends—that is, the poetry of the *Vita nuova* ends—with the words *donne*

mie care. Are these the same ladies to whom he addressed his first *canzone*, "Donne ch'avete intelletto d'amore"—or do the words refer merely to the two "donne gentili" who had asked him to send them some of his poetry at the beginning of the chapter?

23. There are exactly twenty-two sighs mentioned in the *Vita nuova:* eleven in the prose and eleven in the poetry. But could this sigh of XLI, which has become a spirit capable of ascending to Heaven (no longer reminding us, that is, of the sickly *spiritelli* of the first part of the book) be a further spiritualization of the sigh which Beatrice's presence invited from those who looked upon her in the famous sonnet of Chapter XXVI? Surely this was a sigh of pure aspiration, untouched by selfish sentimentality.

24. The lover's inability to accept with composure the death of Beatrice, when he had shown in the first *canzone* how eagerly she was desired in Heaven, is criticized sternly, tenderly, and with a touch of humor in a poem written for him by his friend, Cino da Pistoia:

> *Avvegna ched el m'aggia più per tempo*
> *per voi richesto Pietate e Amore*
> *per confortar la vostra grave vita,*
> *non è ancor sì trapassato il tempo*
> *che 'l mio sermon non trovi il vostro core*
> *piangendo star con l'anima smarrita,*
> *fra sè dicendo: "Già sete in ciel gita,*
> *beata gioia, com chiamava il nome!*
> *Lasso me! quando e come*
> *veder vi potrò io visibilmente?"*
> *sì ch'ancora a presente*
> *vi posso fare di conforto aita.*
> *Donque m'odite, poi ch'io parlo a posta*
> *d'Amor, a li sospir ponendo sosta.*

Noi provamo che 'n questo cieco mondo
ciascun si vive in angosciosa noia,
ché in onne avversità ventura 'l tira.
Beata l'alma che lassa tal fondo
e va nel cielo ov'è compiuta gioia,
gioioso 'l cor for di corrotto e d'ira!
Or donque di che 'l vostro cor sospira,
che rallegrar si de' del suo migliore?
Ché Dio, nostro signore,
volse di lei, com'avea l'angel detto,
fare il cielo perfetto.
Per nova cosa onne santo la mira,
ed ella sta davanti a la Salute
ed inver lei parla onne Vertute.

Di che vi stringe 'l cor pianto ed angoscia,
che dovresti d'amor sopragioire,
ch'avete in ciel la mente e l'intelletto?
Li vostri spirti trapassar da poscia
per sua vertù nel ciel; tal è 'l disire,
ch'Amor lassù li pinge per diletto.
O omo saggio, perché sì distretto
vi tien così l'affannoso pensero?
Per suo onor vi chero
ch' a l'egra mente prendiate conforto,
nè aggiate più cor morto
nè figura di morte in vostro aspetto:
perché Dio l'aggia locata fra i soi,
ella tuttora dimora con voi.

Conforto, già, conforto l'Amor chiama,
e Pietà priega "Per Dio, fate resto!":
or inchinate a sì dolce preghera.
Spogliatevi di questa vesta grama,
da che voi sete per ragion richesto;
ché l'omo per dolor more a dispera.
Com voi vedresti poi la bella cera
se v'accogliesse morte in disperanza?
Di sì grave pesanza

traete il vostro core omai, per Dio,
che non sia così rio
ver l'alma vostra, che ancora spera
vederla in cielo e star ne le sue braccia:
donque spene di confortar vi piaccia.

Mirate nel piacer dove dimora
la vostra donna ch'è 'n ciel coronata;
ond'è la vostra spene in paradiso,
e tutta santa omai vostr' innamora,
contemplando nel ciel mente locata.
Lo core vostro per cui sta diviso,
che pinto tene 'n sè beato viso?
Secondo ch'era qua giù meraviglia,
così là su somiglia,
e tanto più quant'è me' conosciuta.
Come fu ricevuta
da gli angeli con dolce canto e riso,
gli spiriti vostri rapportato l'hanno,
che spesse volte quel viaggio fanno.

Ella parla di voi con li beati,
e dice loro: "Mentre ched io fui
nel mondo, ricevei onor da lui,
laudando me nei suo' detti laudati".
E priega Dio, lo signor verace,
che vi conforti sì come vi piace.

In the first stanza Cino shows his familiarity with the last *can-zone* of the *Vita nuova*. His reference to the tears that Dante must still be shedding recalls the opening lines "Li occhi do-lenti . . . ," and the words that he puts into Dante's mouth, "Già sete in ciel gita . . ." are taken from the end of the first stanza: ". . . si n'è gita in ciel subitamente." In Cino's second stanza, where he blames the young lover for not rejoicing over Beatrice's bliss in Heaven, he is reminding him, with the words "Ché Dio . . ./ volse di lei, come avea l'angel detto,/ fare il cielo perfetto," of the beginning of the second stanza of the

first *canzone:* "Angelo clama in divino intelletto/e dice. . . ."
The reproach with which Cino opens stanza three ("How can
you grieve . . . ?") is based on Dante's new-found ability to
travel in spirit to Heaven—obviously an allusion to the last sonnet of the *Vita nuova* which opens: "Oltre la spera che più
larga gira/passa 'l sospiro ch'esce del mio core"; and it is in the
name of Dante's honor that he appeals to his friend to take
comfort and to erase from his face the image of death. In the
next stanza appears a menacing note: such grief as the lover is
indulging in leads to desperation and death—and damnation, for
if he should die in his state of desperation he could hardly hope
to see Beatrice in Heaven. The last stanza of Cino's poem, with
the *congedo,* sounds a note of joy, as he pictures the bliss of
Beatrice and of the angelic beings who have her with them.

In case the reader has occasionally wondered whether my
constant carping at the lover's self-pitying moods is exaggerated, revealing callousness to the sensitivity of a lyrical poet
of the *duecento,* this "sermon," addressed to the young Dante
by his contemporary, and intimate friend, would seem to bear
out my criticism.

25. According to Colin Hardie, "Dante and the Tradition of
Courtly Love" (in *Patterns of Love and Courtesy,* 1966, 31–
40), the poem that Dante was contemplating writing in Chapter XLII, which would contain words never before said about
a lady, was not the *Divine Comedy* but rather the *canzone*
"Amor, tu vedi ben."

26. If the distinction between Dante the author and Dante
the protagonist is seldom made, even less frequently do we find
the suggestion that Dante the author was to any extent critical
of the behavior of his protagonist—as Jefferson Fletcher believes ("The 'True Meaning' of Dante's *Vita Nuova,*" *Romanic Review,* XI, 2, 95–148). Fletcher even recognizes the

humor in Chapter XVIII, sensing that the author was making fun of the young lover. However, he believes that the flaws of the protagonist are merely those that are to be expected of "Noble Youth", and surely does not believe that the protagonist is held up as a warning example.

27. It was stated earlier in reference to Canto V of the *Inferno* that it would be absurd to imagine that the agonizing pity which the Pilgrim felt for Francesca reflected the attitude of Dante the Poet. I would go further and say that the presentation of the Pilgrim in this canto amounts to an indictment of his emotional self-indulgence: when, swooning in pity over Francesca's fate, he falls unconscious to the floor of Hell, his collapse symbolizes the sin of subjecting reason to emotion —which was ultimately the sin of the Lustful (cf. the chapter "A Lesson in Lust" in my forthcoming book of Dante studies). It is true that the weakness shown by the Pilgrim here is that of excessive pity for another person, whereas in the *Vita nuova* it was self-pity in which the lover indulged; but the uncontrollable, uncritical sympathy that the Pilgrim lavished upon Francesca was the same kind of sympathy that the protagonist of the *Vita nuova* had craved for himself. Granted this parallel between the lover throughout the *Vita nuova* and the Pilgrim in his first encounter with the Damned, it could be said, stretching a point or two, that the *Inferno* begins with a recapitulation of the *Vita nuova*—just as the *Vita nuova* ends with an anticipation of the *Divine Comedy*.

28. To speak of the lover's weakness as a canker, as a disease, is of course to present it positively as a thing in itself, as a destructive force. But this weakness can also be seen from a negative point of view: as a great lack, as the result of a great emptiness. The protagonist of the *Vita nuova* lived in a vacuum; except for his feelings, and except for Beatrice as their

stimulus, nothing else existed in his world. I have spoken of the shadowy, nameless city in which he lived, peopled by nameless shadows. His city, which not only is never named but also is never described, did not exist for him—nor did its history, its political concerns, its culture. The people there did not exist for him, or the problems they may have had. He had no neighbors. Given this inner lack of all selfless concerns, he could never have overcome his sentimentality by struggling within himself. The emptiness of which this sentimentality was a result had to be filled by other things; only by becoming aware of the plenitude of creation could he ever see Beatrice as she truly was.

To become aware of the vastness, and the order, of the cosmos will be granted to the Pilgrim in his journey through the realms of the After Life. He will meet with sinners of every stripe, and with heroes, sages and saints; he will be instructed in astronomy, and enter into the Empyrean. The plan of salvation will be explained to him, and he will be given a classification of the variety of sins and of virtues. He will ponder the relationship between Free Will and Predestination; he will learn about Divine Justice and justice on earth, and the relationship that should exist between the Church and the Empire; he will follow through the ages the history of the Church and of the Empire. He will learn at last what Love is, in terms of the Cosmos, and will be able to see Beatrice plain at the summit of the Mountain of Purgatory, before he ascends with her to Paradise, and to the final vision of the Triune God.

To go from the *Vita nuova* through the *Divine Comedy* is to progress from the *inter nos* to the *extra nos* to the *super nos* of St. Bonaventure.

29. Alan M. F. Gunn (*The Mirror of Love*) believes that the *Roman de la Rose* offers a glorification of the lover's quest

for the Rose. More recent critics, however, such as D. W. Robertson, Rosamund Tuve, and J. B. Fleming believe that Jean de Meung is pitilessly indicting the hero. Further corroboration of this opinion will be offered in a forthcoming article by Anna Granville Hatcher, based primarily on a close analysis of the last thousand lines, in which she shows how the literary technique of Jean de Meung (an aspect of the work mainly neglected by the three critics just mentioned) is brought into play to drive home his indictment of the hero—an indictment far crueler than that of the *Vita nuova*.

30. Leo Spitzer ("Bemerkungen zu Dantes 'Vita nuova'," *Travaux du Séminaire de Philologie Romane* I, 162–208, Istamboul, 1937) in a brief discussion of the Latinity of the speeches of the three *spiriti*, notes (p. 174) that the first two speak in relatively correct Latin, while the third (the spirit governing the digestive system) is guilty of several barbarisms: e.g. *Heu miser* for *Heu me miserum*. He assumes, as something obvious, that the crude Latin was deliberately attributed to the least spiritual of the *spiriti* for comic effect.

31. See Singleton "The Use of Latin in the *Vita nuova*," MLN, 1946, pp. 108–112. He quotes Spitzer's article mainly because of the latter's remarks on the Latin used in Chapter XII; he mentions Spitzer's remarks about the Latin in Chapter II, but he is politely hesitant about accepting Spitzer's lighthearted interpretation.

32. That the lover had great difficulty in grasping the sublimity of Beatrice's nature (as the number 9) is humanly quite understandable. Guinizelli who, in his famous *canzone* "Al cor gentil . . . ," had compared the efficacy of a lovely lady to the efficacy of God the Creator, allows himself in the last stanza to be sternly rebuked by God. Thereby, he is confessing good-

naturedly (for surely the polite apology he offers to God is humorously self-deprecatory) that he had been exaggerating the perfection of a lovely lady all along. Dante, however, will not allow the lover to cease struggling to understand the divine in Beatrice, and he rewards him for this effort in the final vision that the reader of the *Vita nuova* is not allowed to see.